Better Together

Better Together

The Future of Presbyterian Mission

SHERRON KAY GEORGE

Geneva Press
Louisville, Kentucky

First edition
Published by Geneva Press
Louisville, Kentucky

10 11 12 13 14 15 16 17 18 19—10 9 8 7 6 5 4 3 2 1

Except as otherwise noted, Scripture quotations are from the New Revised Standard Version of the Bible, copyright © 1989 by the Division of Christian Education of the National Council of the Churches of Christ in the U.S.A., and used by permission. One quotation marked NLT is from the New Living Translation.

Figures 3.1 and 3.2 were originally published in Sherron Kay George, "Local-Global Mission: The Cutting Edge." *Missiology* 28, no. 2 (April 2000): 187–97, and are used with permission.

Figures 1.1 and 4.1 were originally published in Sherron Kay George, "Faithfulness through the Storm: Changing Theology of Mission," in *A History of Presbyterian Missions: 1944–2007*, ed. Scott W. Sunquist and Caroline N. Becker, 85–109 (Louisville, KY: Geneva Press, 2008), and are used with permission.

Book design by Sharon Adams
Cover design by Night & Day Design

Library of Congress Cataloging-in-Publication Data

George, Sherron Kay.
  Better together : the future of Presbyterian mission / Sherron Kay George.
    p. cm.
  Includes bibliographical references (p.   ).
  ISBN 978-0-664-50306-2 (alk. paper)
  1. Presbyterian Church (U.S.A.)—Missions.   2. Missions—Theory.   I. Title.
  BV2570.G458 2010
  266'.5137—dc22

                                                                2009033657

This book is dedicated to
G. Thompson Brown,
Clifton Kirkpatrick,
Marian McClure Taylor,
and
Hunter Farrell,
Who were the Directors of the Presbyterian world mission agency
Under which I have served since 1972.

They were and are friends, mentors, and inspiration to me
And leaders who have molded and guided
Presbyterian mission work in the world.

To these visionaries and all of the mission workers, national staff,
And international and ecumenical partners who have
Served alongside them, I dedicate this book.

Contents

Foreword

*O*ver the past half century, the cutting edge of U.S.-based mission has shifted from large institutionalized mission agencies (both denominational mission boards and parachurch ministries) to the local congregation:

- Missiologist Robert Priest estimates that *2 million* U.S. Christians travel abroad each year on short-term mission trips.[1]
- Much of the prayer focused on God's mission in the world is stimulated and directed when people come together in their local congregation to engage in mission.
- A large and growing portion of the mission-funding decisions made by U.S. Christians occurs in local congregations.

Yet congregational mission leaders—who are often making major decisions on mission funding, prayer, and the sending of short- and long-term mission workers—have not always had the opportunity to "look before they leap" into the remarkably complex Spirit movement they are joining.

Better Together is a book for congregational mission leaders—the Presbyterians who lead mission trips, teach about mission, invite mission speakers, organize mission conferences, and advocate at session meetings for the inclusion of "mission beyond the congregation" in the annual budget. Long-time mission coworker, professor, and missiologist Sherron George offers a highly useful tool to these key mission leaders: a book of profound insight into the biblical theology of how God works in mission—*and how God's missionary plan can shape our own*. George's conclusion—that God created us to be in mission *together*—cuts across the grain of our cultural tendency to engage in "Lone Ranger mission." She proposes a "missionary dialogue" between evangelism and social justice that will enable congregations to increase the effectiveness—and faithfulness—of their mission efforts.

While, in the popular imagination, mission is often portrayed as "remote" and "exotic," George's book reframes God's mission as the overarching, loving work of God in the world in a way that reconnects the global and the local into a more biblical "mission without borders". This reconnection can revitalize a congregation's mission efforts as they begin to "connect the dots" that link what they are learning through their partnership with a Guatemalan Presbyterian congregation with the growing presence of Guatemalan migrant workers in their presbytery.

The PCUSA has long been known as a church that does mission in partnership with Christian partners around the world. Unfortunately, as our denomination's mission efforts have decentralized and thousands of local congregations, rather than the General Assembly Council, have become the primary mission decision-makers, we have not taken partnership with each other very seriously. "Why is it easier for us to work with our global partners than with each other in our own ecclesial body?" she asks.

Better Together breaks important new ground in its reflections on the challenge of U.S. Presbyterians working together in a more coordinated and effective mission partnership. At a time when Presbyterian World Mission is rapidly reshaping its role to create a place for congregational and other mission leaders to coordinate their efforts (www.missioncrossroads.ning.com) and to provide tools for congregations to engage more effectively in God's mission, George has brought together a profound and sensitive study of biblical mission principles with a lifetime of mission practice and has given us a beautiful gift: the opportunity to be more faithful and effective in God's grace-filled mission.

Hunter Farrell

Preface

*H*ave you ever assembled a thousand-piece jigsaw puzzle? When I was a child in North Carolina, my family loved to do puzzles together especially around Christmas. My dad usually worked on the edges. Each of us would choose a certain part of the picture—blue sky, water, green grass, colorful flowers, or an interesting building—and find all the pieces to construct that part. However, we all relentlessly looked at the "big picture" on the box to see how each assembled group fit into the whole. Only with the big picture of the puzzle could we fit the parts together.

As I reflect on four decades as a Presbyterian Church (U.S.A.) mission coworker, I now see that my journey has consisted of little parts of a big picture. As time goes by, the picture I envision grows bigger and bigger.

During the 1970s I worked in fourteen rural congregations in western Brazil. I spent hours driving on dusty roads, enjoying warm Brazilian hospitality and embraces, hearing stories, and leading services in churches and homes. However, absorption in one cozy corner of the world can lead to isolation from the larger religious, political, and economic picture. Like my rural parishioners, I was oblivious to the situation in Brazil's cities under the military government.

When I moved to Manaus, the picture suddenly became urban but included the vast Amazon Basin, with its magnificent jungle and rivers. I encouraged my students to see all of it as their mission field. However, the churches in Manaus are very isolated from the rest of Brazil.

In 1986 the Independent Presbyterian Church of Brazil invited me to teach in their seminary in Londrina, and I became a participant observer of my students and colleagues as they stood in solidarity with the least, analyzed church and society, created Brazilian liturgy, and challenged me as a missionary from what they considered to be an imperialistic country and a dominating culture. My picture was undergoing a radical transformation.

I attentively followed Brazil's evening news and soap operas, passionately discussed Brazilian political and economic issues, and began to view world and U.S. actions and to do theology from the perspective of the Southern hemisphere.

Then in 1995 I sensed God calling me to return to the United States and enter the strange new burnt-orange world of Texas and Austin Presbyterian Theological Seminary as Professor of Evangelism and Mission. In this new location, I found myself bonding with our Hispanic and international students and learning to look at the world's needs, the global churches' gifts, and our culture through their eyes. During my time in Austin, I also lectured in Senegal, China, Cuba, and Lithuania. I had become a bicultural member of the global faith community, and my picture could never again be limited to one country or continent.

In 2001 no one was surprised when I returned to live in Brazil as a PC(USA) mission coworker, with the jobs of theological education consultant and regional liaison for South America. As liaison I seek to help bridge the distance between the national offices in Louisville (Ky.) and PC(USA) congregations and mission personnel and partner churches on the field.

Now my picture includes Argentina, Bolivia, Brazil, Chile, Colombia, Ecuador, Peru, Uruguay, and Venezuela, plus seminaries in Costa Rica and Cuba. Because of my growing passion and interest in the whole continent, I loved the movie *Motorcycle Diaries* (2004). It portrays the journey of two young Argentines, Che Guevara and Alberto Granado, who left Buenos Aires in 1952 on motorcycles, with Venezuela as their destination. What an amazing journey through the pampas, Andes, Pacific coast, desert, rivers, and jungle! On the road, they perceived the suffering of the people and acquired a new social awareness and perspective that transformed their lives and aspirations.

Though I don't ride a motorcycle, my world has expanded. In addition to the Presbyterian parts of the picture, I am getting to know the Roman Catholic Church, a Lutheran seminary, and Pentecostals at ecumenical gatherings. For instance, in Buenos Aires I met a dynamic Quechua woman in lovely typical dress who is the Minister of Justice in Bolivia. This is a major step in a country where indigenous peoples have been exploited and marginalized for five centuries; yet now it has an elected indigenous president.

I am a global Christian, living and focusing on the South American part of the picture, which includes a vibrant passion for Brazilian soccer. All of the Americas are on my screen. While deepening my roots in South America and becoming increasingly ecumenical, I have a special concern for the PC(USA)'s participation in the many pieces of God's local-global mission. I am proud to be a part of our denominational agency, Presbyterian World Mission.

Presbyterians *do* mission! It's in our blood. But we can and must do it better. What are our cutting edges? For most of our history we have entrusted the national church to do mission in our name. Now local churches are getting their hands dirty and rediscovering the joys and pains of working with and for others who hurt. One-quarter of Presbyterian congregations sent out at least one work team to help with disaster relief in the United States in the last two years. Many have international presbytery partnerships. But is it *either* denominational agencies *or* local congregations doing mission? Why can´t local churches, presbyteries, the national mission agency, and other mission agencies work together for the greater good? Do we need to split ourselves into opposing interest groups? Why don't the streams majoring in evangelism, compassion, and prophetic justice dialogue with one another? Who is helped when we compete and tear one another down? How can we learn from one another, support one another, and be united in our mission efforts? Can we learn to focus on the big picture of God's mission rather than on the small parts? How can we fit the pieces of this mission puzzle together into a whole? What would it look like to value those who are working on other parts? Where can we find guidance in the quest for new patterns?

The Epistle to the Ephesians presents some possible insights and answers to these questions. This letter invites us to expand our vision and to unite many diverse parts in the big picture of God's mission. The churches who received this letter faced a situation that has many similarities to ours today. Probably it was written after 70 CE, when the Roman Empire destroyed the nation of Israel and the temple in Jerusalem.[1] Christians found themselves in a new world with new references and a plurality of cultures. The church was going through its first major paradigm shift. The majority were no longer Palestinian Jews but were now in a Greco-Roman world, and they were Gentile or non-Jewish. Christians were divided and struggling to understand their identity. Rigid institutional structures in society were influencing the nascent church. And people were caught up in speculations about angels and demons.

What shall the church do with all these changes and cultural diversity? How do Christians break down the walls and barriers of hostility between ethnic groups? What is the nature and mission of the church in a world where evil is a reality? These were the issues in the Letter to the Ephesians.

Our situation today is similar. The global church is going through another major demographic shift. The majority church is now non-Western and no longer centered in the North Atlantic. The demographic center of the church is in the Southern hemisphere and is increasingly multicultural. Many ethnic, religious, and theological conflicts and tensions divide us in the world and in the church.

The first three chapters of the book will deal with our mission problems, practices, and contexts. Each chapter will begin with a case study. The book will ask some key questions that we all have about how the PC(USA) is doing mission in the world today. These questions will engage and compel us. The book might be called a missiology of questions. What is mission today? Who is engaged in mission? How are all the players connected? How do we maintain our integrity and work together rather than give in to competition? How do we relate local and global mission work in our globalized world? How do we integrate evangelism, compassion, and justice? Answering these questions will take years of study, reflection, experience, and dialogue together. We must be open to listen to one another. Together we can identify our cutting edges. In fact, by posing the questions, I think that we already are beginning to deal with some cutting edges.

After exploring these thorny issues related to our mission practice, we will turn to a more intentional biblical reflection in chapter 4. Some lessons from Ephesians will shed light on possible solutions and ways of doing mission better while doing it together as the body of Christ. There are many ways for each of us to be faithful in the parts of God's plan entrusted to us.

The outline for this book developed in a conversation with Hunter Farrell, the Director of Presbyterian World Mission, during the PC(USA) mission consultation in Dallas in January 2008. The final document of that consultation, "An Invitation to Expanding Partnership in God's Mission" (Appendix B), and the resulting movement confirm the need for this book. Following the consultation, I lectured on holistic mission at Shandon Presbyterian Church in Columbia (S.C.) and shared the book project with their mission pastor, Steve Earl, who has encouraged me in the project. Some months later Hunter invited several staff members of World Mission to present the proposal to David Maxwell, Executive Editor of Geneva Press. David offered valuable insights, the group brainstormed, and we came up with the idea of inviting some readers to accompany me and offer comments and suggestions. I am grateful to Hunter and to David for their support of this project. I also want to thank publicly my readers Michael Parker and Marian McClure Taylor, who carefully read the entire manuscript, engaged in missiological reflection with me, and offered extremely helpful suggestions. I am also grateful to Art Beals and Tim Dobbins for their thoughtful comments and to my immediate supervisor Maria Arroyo for generously allowing me to dedicate much time to writing.

Better Together: The Future of Presbyterian Mission can be a valuable tool for mission education and mobilization by helping us recognize and embrace the movement of God's Spirit in the world. The book honors the integrity of the gospel, of God's mission, and of the body of Christ. My fervent prayer is that renewal and mission convergence will come as we discover new connections and fullness in God's mission, which includes many parts, participants, and places. I pray that we will be empowered to celebrate the breadth of what each of us does in the service of Christ's name. Let us give thanks for the connectedness of the vital structures that make up the whole body of Christ and make a profound commitment to togetherness in one mission. I wish you God's grace and courage as you enlarge your vision and participation in the big picture of mission that is always better together.

Sherron Kay George
Curitiba, PR, Brazil
Pentecost 2009

Chapter 1

What Is Mission Today?

Many Parts, One Mission: Integrating Evangelism, Compassion, and Justice

The new pastor was encouraged by all of the activities of the urban 300-member congregation but sensed a certain fragmentation and isolation, maybe even rivalry among the many groups and committees. She decided to plan a retreat for the members to reflect and play together and was pleased at the number of folks who signed up to attend.

After a good time of worship and fellowship together, she gathered everyone for an open conversation in the morning session. The topic she chose was "mission." She decided that it was best to see where the members were in their conceptions and practices, so she simply began with the question "What is mission today for you?" The first person to speak was the chair of the Mission Committee. "It is what the five mission workers we support in other countries do. We pledge to support them financially and pray for their mission work." A young person responded, "The youth group goes on a mission trip to Mexico one year and another trip to help rebuild damaged houses in the U.S.A. the next year." Giggling, the girl next to him replied, "I remember last year when one young Mexican asked us how youth do evangelism in the United States, and I responded in shock that we don't."

An outspoken member continued, "That is the problem with our church. We don't know how to do evangelism anymore. It is the dirty e-word. So we don't grow. Evangelism is the most important part of mission. We must fulfill the Great Commission." Quickly a member of the Outreach Committee remarked, "Yes, we do, but we don't call it evangelism. We receive new members." Someone asked, "Is being a greeter on Sunday morning doing mission?" A new Peruvian member shyly added, "When I first arrived, I saw someone from this congregation deliver a loaf of bread to a doctor in my neighborhood who had visited worship, but I never received one." Another person reflected, "I think receiving leaders from our partner churches to share their witness and to teach us is what some people call mission-in-reverse." Then someone shouted, "Social justice is the essence of mission. Look at the prophets and Jesus' declaration in Luke 4 about liberating the oppressed." He then shared that the Presbyterian Peace Fellowship trains and sends volunteers to Colombia in a ministry of accompaniment, being with our partners who suffer in their struggle for human rights. Immediately another person said, "I have never heard of Presbyterian Peace Fellowship, but Presbyterian Frontier Fellowship supports groups in Central Asia who are planting new Christian communities." Someone added, "Matthew 25 says we should feed the hungry and clothe the needy, and we do that together with other religious groups." People then started mentioning local soup kitchens, Habitat for Humanity, disaster assistance, and other ministries of compassion.

At the end it was clear that everyone had a definition of mission and an emphatic preference for what they felt was important. However, many folks had no real understanding of or appreciation for the opinions and practices of others. The pastor closed by reading Ephesians 4:1–6 and asking, "Is the church an organization of individuals and special-interest groups who do mission their own way and ignore or judge those who do it other ways? Or could we all be members of one team who encourage, affirm, support, and need one another as we engage in the many parts of God's one mission together? Might there be a way for us to renew our organizational structures and deepen our dialogue to promote more interaction and unity in mission?

"Let's start our session tomorrow morning with those questions. This afternoon our Brazilian fellowship will be coaching us in our soccer match to pass the ball as in a coordinated ballet. There will be other group and individual sports activities. Also several big jigsaw puzzles have been started in the dining room. Let's have fun together."

How many definitions do Presbyterians have for mission? How do folks who engage in mission in very different ways relate to each other in and beyond the PC(USA) and in the world? Could we do mission better together? Can we learn to work cooperatively and even become partners in mission?

What Is Holistic Mission?

When I was growing up, I savored lots of fresh tomato sandwiches—on white bread, of course. Peanut butter and grape jelly sandwiches too—on white bread. It was only later that I discovered the nutritional value of whole-grain bread and cereals. My niece recently told me that she was twelve years old before she ever had white bread! Now I know all about complex carbs and mostly eat whole-grain breads, rice, and cereals. And I know that a complete diet combines carbohydrates, proteins, and fruits and vegetables of all colors.

Diet and physical activities go together. In exercises, I have traveled a similar path. First, I included only walking or swimming: cardiovascular training. Then I discovered water aerobics with lots of fun accessories. My trainer convinced me that I also need weight training. And stretching certainly comes before and after all of the above. I try to complete my program by using a Pilates or yoga tape at least once a week. I have an exercise tape called "Total Body Workout." Once I took a class on holistic gymnastics. My goal now is to have a balanced diet and a complete exercise program.

From the Hebrew Scriptures and especially from non-Western cultures, I have gleaned how to think about life holistically, not to separate body and soul, physical and spiritual. Reformed Christians from Africa have taught me about the importance of holistic or balanced living, in which nothing in life is under-utilized and nothing is neglected. Fullness of life is important not only with food and exercise, but also in mission. Holism challenges the general imbalance in our lives and in our mission. My personal journey toward integration in God's holistic mission has been a process of learning from Latin Americans and others that the realm of God's kingdom covers every area of life. I came out of a very evangelical background that emphasized evangelism, one's vertical personal relationship with the Lord Jesus, and the spiritual aspects of mission. The first time I heard the term "holistic" in reference to mission as a "unitary, indivisible whole" was from Orlando Costas in Montreat, North Carolina. He said: "The true test of mission is not whether we proclaim, make disciples, or engage in social, economic, and political liberation, but whether we are capable of integrating all three in a comprehensive, dynamic, *and consistent* witness. We need to pray that the Lord will . . . liberate us *for* wholeness and integrity in mission."[1] Little did I realize that thirty years later I would still be thinking and writing about the ideas he planted in my mind.

While teaching at the seminary in Londrina, Brazil, in the late 1980s, I started learning about liberation theology. It was born in Latin America as a missionary theology that took seriously the socioeconomic context of poverty and injustice and insisted that evangelization could not occur in a vacuum. These theologians used political language to express the two complementary dimensions of mission: personal and social transformation. I was converted to the equal importance of this second dimension.

The person who epitomizes holistic mission for me is C. René Padilla. I remember when I went to the lovely Kairos Community outside Buenos Aires to meet him and spend an afternoon talking about mission. Padilla insists that the fullness of mission includes evangelism and discipleship, partnership and unity, development and justice. It is "centered in a prophetic lifestyle" and points to "Jesus Christ as the Lord over the totality of life, to the universality of the church, and to the interdependence of human beings in the world."[2] What most amazes me is the deep passion he has both for evangelism and for social justice. Frequently people in churches in the United States choose to emphasize one or the other. For Padilla, they are distinct, like two wings of a bird, but integrally connected. Our cutting edge is experiencing the connection, the interaction, the convergence, the wholeness, the fullness of mission.

In Buenos Aires I also encountered José Míguez Bonino. For him, mission begins with the Trinitarian dialogue between Father, Son, and Spirit, and we are included in God's "missionary dialogue." He encourages us to emphasize both the unity of God's one mission and the distinctions of its dimensions. Consider all the ways we participate in the liberating and evangelizing task. For example, look at the case study at the beginning of this chapter. Notice the particularity of each task mentioned and the attitude of the speaker. Their kind of mission seems to be the best. Bonino helped me see that often we have "failed to participate in the fullness" of God's mission. A better understanding of each part in the context of the "total 'mission' of God can guide us to correct our mistakes."[3] We have an opportunity today to reintegrate the many pieces.

When I taught at Austin Presbyterian Theological Seminary, I used South African David J. Bosch's *Transforming Mission*, which speaks of a "comprehensive," "integral," or "total" view of salvation. Bosch admonishes us to "minister to people in their *total* need" and "involve individual as well as society, soul *and* body, present *and* future in our ministry of salvation."[4] For him, like whole multigrain bread, "Mission is a multifaceted ministry, in respect of witness, service, justice, healing, reconciliation, liberation, peace, evangelism, fellowship, church planting, contextualization, and much more."[5] By connecting our dots in mission, we can eat healthy whole-grain mission.

My Roman Catholic colleagues Steve Bevans and Roger Schroeder propose "prophetic dialogue" as a model for this "single but complex reality." I suggest "evangelistic and prophetic dialogue." Recognizing the multidimensional nature of mission, they suggest six key components: (1) witness and proclamation; (2) liturgy, prayer, and contemplation; (3) justice, peace, and the integrity of creation; (4) interreligious dialogue; (5) inculturation;[6] and (6) reconciliation. The six elements are "all distinct from one another and yet intricately intertwined as well" because "there is *one* mission: the mission of God that is shared, by God's grace, by the church."[7]

A recent important book is *Mission in the Twenty-first Century: Exploring the Five Marks of Global Missions*, edited by Andrew Walls and Cathy Ross, with essays from voices in the majority world that "urge us, disturb us, encourage us, and challenge us." The Five Marks "are neither a perfect nor a complete definition of mission, [but] they do form a good working basis for a holistic approach to mission." The Five Marks call for Christians

1. To proclaim the good news of the kingdom.
2. To teach, baptize, and nurture new believers.
3. To respond to human need by loving service.
4. To seek to transform unjust structures of society.
5. To strive to safeguard the integrity of creation and sustain and renew the life of the earth.[8]

In what follows I combine the first two marks into one part: evangelism and discipleship. I then treat the third mark under compassionate service. I combine the fourth and fifth marks because I see the ecological crisis as a social justice issue.

Three Essential and Related Parts of God's One Holistic Mission

Do you and people in your congregation or mission group truly believe that there is one mission—God's holistic mission? When you are engaged in some particular aspect of mission, are you aware of the fact that you are part of a much bigger picture? Jesus demonstrated this awareness when talking about God's reign. He defined his mission in Luke 4: "The Spirit of the Lord . . . has anointed me to bring good news to the poor. He has sent me to proclaim release to the captives and recovery of sight to the blind, to let the oppressed go free, to proclaim the year of the Lord's favor." Jesus' mission included proclamation of the good news (evangelism), compassion, and justice. Do you affirm all three of these essential distinct interrelated parts of mission that are practiced in accord with different gifts and situations?

My cutting-edge proposal in this book is that a "missionary dialogue" between people involved in ministries of evangelism, compassionate service, and social justice that mutually feeds, complements, and corrects one another should guide the PC(USA). Unity and a common witness will bring renewal to all. However, to embrace the fullness of God's holistic mission, we must understand and honor each distinct part (see fig. 1.1).[9]

FINAL GOAL OF ALL MISSION IS GOD'S GLORY AND REALM OF LOVE, PEACE, AND JUSTICE

GOD'S MISSION OF RESTORATION, SALVATION, LIBERATION, AND RECONCILIATION

is the foundation and source of the mission of the church.

MISSION, *therefore,*

is the identity, reason, and purpose of the church;

is the responsibility of every baptized Christian;

is done in partnership with God for God's glory in 6 continents by the church in 6 continents;

is local-global and holistic (integral), without compartmentalization, polarization, or dichotomy.

Therefore, God's mission sends the church into the world with at least three roles and always includes and mixes three aspects:

EVANGELISM (Church as messenger)	COMPASSIONATE SERVICE (Church as servant/diakonia)	SOCIAL JUSTICE (Church as prophet)
with bold humility and respect by lifestyle, words, attitudes, and actions:	with mercy by actions, attitudes, dialogue, lifestyle, and sometimes words that explain why	by political actions, attitudes, dialogue, lifestyle, and sometimes words that explain why
Verbal Proclamation of "Good News"		
Faithful Witness and Dialogue	Emergency Crisis Assistance	Reconciliation and Peace Building
Faith Commitment and Sharing	Care for Displaced Persons	Human Rights
Inviting/Calling	Human Needs: Dignity, Food, Shelter,	Advocacy
Hospitality—Welcoming/Receiving	Health, Education, Living Wage	Solidarity with the Poor
Initiation/Belonging/Baptismal Calling		End to Violence, Terrorism, and War
Assimilating New Members and Gifts	Interfaith Dialogue and Cooperation	Economic Justice
New Church Development	Formation of Coalitions and Alliances	Just Distribution of Power and Systems
		Ecological Justice
Intention: "Life in all its fullness"	Intention: Meeting human needs	Public Policy
Conversion/Discipleship/Growth	Capacity-building/Empowerment	Interfaith Dialogue and Cooperation
	Healing and Building Sustainable	
Confessing Jesus as Lord	Communities	Intention: Social Transformation
Building Up the Body of Believers		
Developing Disciples, the Church	Showing what God's reign means for	Showing what God's reign means for
	the whole world	the whole world

Fig. 1.1. God's Holistic Mission

Evangelism Is One Part

The Presbyterian Church (U.S.A.) *Book of Order* tells us that the church is a messenger "called to be Christ's faithful evangelist going into the world [and across the street], making disciples."[10] We must do this with bold humility and respect for the freedom and beliefs of those who hear our message. Our lifestyle, attitudes, and actions must be consistent with the gospel and prepare the way for our words. Evangelism is most often the verbal proclamation, communication, or sharing in word and deed of the good news of the love and saving grace of God. Jesus' ministry clearly demonstrates that evangelization includes a gracious invitation (without pressure, imposition, or manipulation) and a call to decision and discipleship. Again, the *Book of Order* says, "The Church is called to present the claims of Jesus Christ, leading persons to repentance, acceptance of him as Savior and Lord, and new life as his disciples."[11]

Through faithful witness and discerning dialogue, every baptized Christian and every local congregation has the responsibility of sharing our faith commitment with others. Some people are more gifted for verbal proclamation than others. We learn in 1 Corinthians 12 that we have different gifts, which come from the one Spirit. Wholeness is the complementary nature of those gifts within the church. In addition to a verbal proclamation, the evangelistic ministry of the church includes the practices of hospitality, inviting, welcoming, and receiving new persons into the faith community. We follow the example of Philip, who invited the cynical Nathanael, "Come and see" (John 1:46). Important questions to ask ourselves are these: Do new people "feel" welcomed in our midst? Are we a welcoming congregation?

In holistic evangelism, followers of Jesus Christ are assimilated and initiated into a community where they experience a sense of belonging, a baptismal calling to mission, and nurturing with the recognition and development of their gifts. When we understand evangelism from the perspective of God's holistic mission, we earnestly desire "life in all its fullness" for all (John 10:10 NLT). Evangelism results in personal transformation or conversion, an intimate personal faith experience, discipleship, and a lifelong process of growth and service in a local faith community, which is part of the church universal.

Evangelism leads both to new church development and to church growth and maturity. The church today is worldwide, present in virtually every country in the world. But the evangelistic task is not complete. The church in every place has the primary responsibility for evangelism in that place. Where are the frontiers today? Wherever people have not heard or understood the gospel of Jesus as good news that gives meaning to their lives and brings healing to their brokenness. Wherever there is no indigenous church, the message must be communicated with authenticity and relevance. In the Western context this often means reaching out to postmodern and secular people, who may be resistant to the institutional church yet seeking a spiritual experience. Jesus is building his church (Matt. 16:18), which is a living organism with institutional structures in need of continual reform to better equip it for transforming mission.

However, we must always remember that the church is only an instrument, witness, and sign of God's mission and reign. The goal of God's mission is captured in the words of the Lord's Prayer: "Your kingdom come" (Matt. 6:10). Mission is for the glory of God and the establishment of God's reign on earth. By bearing faithful witness to Christ, the church glorifies God. The church, however, is not the end that we seek. Nor is proselytism the end. Mission activity and church growth are not the ends. A closed inward-focused group for fellowship is not the end. The church is composed of those whom God calls and gathers for worship, nurture, preparation, and fellowship in order to be scattered and sent back into the world to evangelize and engage in compassionate service and social justice. The church exists for mission to the glory of God.

Compassionate Service Is One Part

In addition to proclaiming the good news, Jesus engaged in mission by feeding the hungry and by "curing every disease and every sickness. When he saw the crowds, he had compassion for them, because they were harassed and helpless, like sheep without a shepherd" (Matt. 9:35–36). He practiced ministries of healing, wholeness, and compassionate service, ministering to the total needs of the whole person, and said that when we feed the hungry, welcome strangers, offer clothing, care for the sick, and visit prisoners, we do it to Jesus himself (Matt. 25:35–36).

The church is not only a messenger; it must also be a servant active in the ministry of *diakonia* (serving others in need). In a world of brokenness and suffering, the church reaches out with mercy and compassion, responding to the needs around us in concrete actions accompanied by coherent attitudes and lifestyles and sometimes by words that explain why we take these actions.

Because of our common humanity with all of God's creatures, we must reach out in compassion wherever there is human need for welcome, dignity, self-respect, food, clothing, shelter, safety, health, education, or a living wage. Mission begins at home in our own land, where people suffer from domestic violence, sexual abuse, abandonment, loneliness, depression, and chemical dependencies. A vital part of the church's mission is emergency crisis assistance near and far away. We must be sensitive and open to the needs and calamities of the multitudes of displaced persons, survivors, refugees, and immigrants in our nation and world. We cannot ignore the global food crisis and the AIDS crisis in Africa, as well as the conditions that cause deaths from malaria and tuberculosis.

There are denominational and ecumenical agencies that help coordinate and channel our aid in these ministries. To minister effectively to the many human needs around us, ecumenical and interfaith dialogue and cooperation are necessary. This leads to the formation of coalitions, networks, and alliances with religious people and others of good will in governmental and nongovernmental agencies.

Through compassionate service we commit to meeting human need, capacity building, personal empowerment of individuals and groups, protection, and building sustainable communities. Our desire is for the healing and wholeness of all God's creatures and the well-being of all creation. As Donal Dorr explains, the ministries of "people involved in the provision of health services, education, social services, community development, ecology work, empowerment of women and of the poor or marginalized groups, and those involved in education for human rights, democracy and civic responsibility" are concerned primarily with promoting the values of God's reign, which brings fullness of life. Their work complements those whose primary concern is building up the church.[12] In turn, the church is built up in order to go out and serve the world in the name of Christ.

Social Justice Is One Part

Contemplate reflectively the words of Stephen Knisely, a Christian theologian: "As we engage in compassionate service, it becomes apparent that the basic problem of human suffering may not lie in the individual but in the structures of society. . . . Justice is the Christian's response to the systemic problem of society."[13]

Many Presbyterian congregations in the United States do a notable local or global mission work as social service or assistance. However, they have not yet addressed the root causes and sought cures through political action for social justice. The church is not only a messenger and a servant; it is also called to be a prophet, "engaging in the struggle to free people from sin, fear, oppression, hunger, and injustice."[14] We have read about the prophets in the Hebrew Scriptures and the biblical concept of Jubilee (Lev. 25:23–34). Surely we have seen the commitment of Jesus to social and economic justice and the total liberation of those suffering from economic, political, and spiritual oppression, especially in Luke's Gospel. We see Zacchaeus in Luke 19, part of the empire's system of unjust tax collectors, and his act of restorative justice toward all he has defrauded when he has a personal encounter with Jesus.

The civil rights and anticolonialist movements of the 1950s and 1960s, the liberation theologies in the 1970s, and more recently the antiapartheid movement and the antiglobalization movements have helped us recognize political action as a part of God's holistic mission. Today alternative proposals for a fair globalization seek the just distribution of opportunities and power and the reformation of economic structures and systems for the sake of all participants. Around the world are movements against toxic wastes, which affect many vulnerable groups. It is easy to affirm justice, but prophetic dialogue must lead to political action for structural change and social transformation that begins in our own land and extends around the planet.

As in the ministries of evangelism and compassionate service, there are many practices included in mission as social justice. Mission not only reduces welfare rolls but also reforms welfare and health-care systems and enables the self-development and empowerment of the poor. It leads Christians to deal honestly with all forms of institutional racism and discrimination. Participation in God's holistic mission leads us to seek an end to all forms of violence (e.g., domestic violence, terrorism, and wars) through multilateral dialogues and joint efforts. In response to the pleas of those who hear our groaning creation, which suffers from global warming and pollution, we join in God's mission, which promotes the integrity of creation and ecological justice. The National Association of Evangelicals (NAE) surveyed evangelical leaders, and "creation care" was one of the top five issues of concern.[15] The present economic crisis can teach us in the United States the importance of simpler lifestyles, which challenge the greed, waste, and unrestrained consumerism that characterize our culture. Mission means reeducation and change in our food and energy consumption. The global food crisis and demands for alternative sources of energy require a response that begins with our habits, but also recognizes the root causes and seeks food security for all.

Reconciliation and peace building are among the most important needs in the world. This is urgent in Iraq, Afghanistan, Sudan, and Israel/Palestine/West Bank. The Presbyterian Church of Egypt has a strategic role in building peace both in Africa and in the Middle East today, as it has historically. The Presbyterian Church in Colombia helps us understand the cost and importance of mission as defending human rights and as advocacy. These are major objectives of the PC(USA) congregations that network with Presbyterians in Israel/Palestine and Colombia.

The Colombia Accompaniment Program, now in its fifth year, arose from a request by the Presbyterian Church of Colombia. Their country has suffered four decades of violent internal conflict, which has been exacerbated over time by an illicit drug trade. In the midst of this violence, the Presbyterian Church of Colombia speaks out against human rights abuses—and for this it faces continued harassment. The program is a ministry of presence with the churches and with the displaced communities and human rights leaders with whom they work. Accompaniers stand in solidarity and spiritual support with the churches and the displaced communities, while providing "international eyes" to what is going on and any threats received by the church or those it serves. Many accompaniers come away with an invigorated sense of what it means to be church. The primary goal is to be a presence of solidarity, to see and be seen, with the benefit of increasing awareness for accompaniers and, through them, our U.S. churches and the broader society. Witness for Peace delegations also provide opportunities to visit and learn about Colombia. One delegation took participants into Colombia's rain forest to meet with peace communities whose traditional small-scale farming is being threatened by agribusiness.

We partner with others as advocates for changes that address the root causes of needs. Reverend Dora Arce, from the Presbyterian and Reformed Church in Cuba, suggests that a vital missional activity of Presbyterians in the United States on behalf of our partner churches is advocacy in the halls of our U.S. government in favor of changes in public policy. The PC(USA) Cuba network has pressured U.S. authorities to end the trade embargo and to pass a Freedom to Travel to Cuba Act that includes all Americans. For the majority church in the Global South, solidarity with the poor is spontaneous. To be Christian companions by standing in solidarity with others for structural and personal justice and change is a cutting-edge issue for us in the North. In our efforts to show what God's reign of peace and justice means for the whole world, we often find support from unlikely people and groups.

If the intention of evangelism is personal transformation, the intention of justice is social transformation. All realms of life are transformed by God. The gospel addresses the totality of life. This is why mission includes evangelism, compassion, and justice. Sadly, we all too often struggle to fully understand, affirm, appreciate, and support people who engage in one of these essential parts that is different from the one to which we are committed. Our typical attitude to other parts of God's mission is indifference. We compartmentalize too much. Why can't we see the interconnections between the pieces of the puzzle? Can we become partners with folks very different from us? Is mission convergence possible?

Integration and Convergence in God's Holistic Mission

One problem we have is that we don't really know one another. I heard a woman involved in social justice say, "I have only met around five evangelicals in my life." For this reason, Presbyterians often fail to see the wholeness of God's mission. My sense is that convergence can be very liberating and empowering for all of us. For this reason I encourage an ongoing missionary dialogue between those who practice evangelism, compassionate service, and social justice. This dialogue will take courage and a willingness to get to know people with whom we may disagree, but this is necessary if we are to overcome our polarizations.

To facilitate this missionary dialogue, the words of John Stott are helpful: "As partners [social action and evangelism] belong to each other and yet are independent of each other. Each stands on its own feet in its own right alongside the other. Neither is a means to the other, or even a manifestation of the other. For each is an end in itself. Both are expressions of unfeigned love."[16] René Padilla states that "evangelism and social responsibility are inseparable" and that as long as both "are regarded as essential to mission, we need no rule of thumb to tell us which comes first and when."[17] I invite you to become dialogue partners with others in mission. Begin by focusing together on the fullness of God's one mission.

Mission is the totality of God's work in the whole creation, at the service of the fullness of God's realm. Salvation addresses the whole person and seeks fullness for all areas of human life: spiritual, existential, psychological, physical, material, social, economic, and political. We cannot ignore the personal, social, or cosmic and ecological dimensions or the historical context of mission. By our one baptism all Christians are called to a common witness to the realm of God. All forms of witness are equal. All mission activities are indispensable parts of the whole. However, all are partial and incomplete. When we engage in a missionary dialogue, integrate our efforts, and partner with others, our participation in God's mission and the manifestation of God's realm both become fuller and more complete. Persons, churches, and mission organizations engaging in this dialogue can overcome reductionisms, divisive priorities, dichotomies, fragmentation, and competition in mission.

The rich diversity of gifts in the body of Christ and the challenging complexity of situations and needs in the world lead baptized Christians, congregations, and mission agencies to engage in the overlapping ministries of evangelism, compassionate service, and social justice at different places and moments in times. These aspects of holistic mission are not competitive or mutually exclusive. We need all three. Each must honor and be accompanied by the others. Practitioners, Vera White says, must "walk hand in hand, complementing and reinforcing each other."[18] We need each other. Christians who constantly practice personal evangelism and those who habitually send letters to their representatives in Congress in advocacy of human rights need each other. Our missionary dialogue can lead to mutual support and mutual correction, as we celebrate our different ministries.

One of the most vivid examples of the delightful harmony of missionary dialogue is the imaginative portrayal of the Trinity in *The Shack*, by William P. Young. The joyful and loving relationship of the large black woman called Elousia or Papa, the Hebrew carpenter Jesus, and the small ever-present Asian woman called Sarayu are especially evident in their meals together. Relationships of love and respect among them and with human beings and creation are the basis of everything. The division of labor of the three persons of the Trinity as they carry out the mission of restoration, reconciliation, and healing in the life of Mackenzie demonstrates the unity in diversity of God's mission action.[19]

In an increasingly divided and polarized church, we must open ourselves to find points of convergence that bring us closer to persons, congregations, mission groups, and denominational agencies understanding and practicing mission in ways different from ours. Let me share five reasons for integration.

1. *Evangelism is a meaningful part of God's mission in and of itself, but it can be reduced to "pie in the sky by and by" when not accompanied by a concern for human suffering.* If a church is only interested in growing numerically or attracting new members, it can become an ingrown social club alienated from the homeless people on the streets and the poor in its city, folks without adequate jobs or housing. People all around us and around the world are suffering. We simply cannot ignore the material and social needs of people. We can only evangelize those who are hungry or in deep pain by first offering medical care and proper nourishment and hygienic living conditions. Yes, evangelism is essential, but we cannot do it like a horse with blinders.

The sermon I heard Orlando Costas, the Puerto Rican pastor, preach nearly thirty years ago was entitled "Eternal Life before Death." He encouraged us to begin living the life that Jesus offers now while we are alive. It was not many years before he succumbed to cancer at the age of forty-five. He insisted that the language we use in sharing the good news cannot only be "spiritual" and in reference solely to "heaven." Salvation is not just an idea, but especially a living experience of faith. It is not simply a future promise, but especially a present dynamic reality, Costas taught us, as he combated a terrible disease.

Orlando Costas died prematurely, but not before he began to live eternal life on earth. His former students at the Latin American Biblical Seminary in Costa

Rica said that he was creative in the classroom and powerful in the pulpit, but that he also participated with them in sports, games, serenades, excursions, and telling jokes. He taught them and us that the good news must be relevant in our day-to-day lives and in our concrete historical context, with all its problems and suffering. Costas challenges us to keep the two-thirds of humankind who are deprived of the essentials of life always before us. We cannot be oblivious to the pain in the world and in the lives of those we want to evangelize.

2. *Compassionate service is a meaningful part of God's mission in and of itself, but it can be reduced to temporary Band-Aids when not accompanied by social transformation.* We must refrain from "charity" that might harm people by causing dependency. I think of the woman I see Sunday after Sunday, sitting on the church's steps and nursing her child, who now is old enough to extend his hand. The coins given cause the little one to grow up with no human dignity or self-respect. We are truly compassionate when we look beyond the immediate needs or requests of individuals and impact the structures of society that can provide long-term solutions. People need housing, jobs, education, and professional help. Many youth participate in house-building projects. Artisans need opportunities to sell their goods directly. A PC(USA) mission worker empowers Peruvian artisans in a fair-trade program. Small businesses need start-up loans. Summer mission trips to join the struggle of migrant farm workers near to home can open our eyes to their situation and long-term needs.

In the human response to complex emergencies, those who engage in compassionate service through relief and development often take additional steps toward addressing root causes and accompanying people who seek just and sustainable community development and transformation. Have there been structural changes in New Orleans to empower the survivors and prevent another Katrina? Are mission groups taking practical steps to provide adequate sanitation systems and safe drinking water for people suffering from preventable diseases in the Southern hemisphere?

Roberto Zwetsch, my friend and colleague in the Evangelical Church of Lutheran Confession in Brazil (IECLB), published a book entitled *Missão como com-paixão.*[20] In Portuguese compassion literally means "with passion." The IECLB has very strong diaconal service ministries. Roberto is supportive of them, but he never sees them without the component of social transformation. He teaches us to minister to human needs while asking questions about the root causes. What changes need to be made in order for more jobs to be available? What can be done so that small farmers are not squeezed out by large landowners? Roberto and his students have developed relationships with a camp of landless Brazilians in an effort to provide adequate education for their children and to speed up the government's program of land reform.

3. *Social justice is a meaningful part of God's mission in and of itself, but it can be reduced to problem solving when not accompanied by the invitation to follow Jesus Christ.* Every coin has two sides. This does not mean that every social action is accompanied by an altar call or even an altar! There is no one-to-one correspondence. It means that our social actions are part of the big picture of holistic mission, which includes sharing the call to follow Jesus. Everything comes at the appropriate moment.

Compassionate service and social justice should be done for their own sake because of the dignity of human beings and *not* as instruments or means of evangelization. We give without expecting or demanding anything in return. Therefore, Christians often participate in soup kitchens or advocacy on behalf of victims of domestic violence, and feel no need to give a verbal witness to their faith. However, when people ask why we do it, or when we discern that the situation is appropriate, we share our personal testimony or invite others to "come and see." We do not have to hide our faith commitment. We seek opportunities to invite others to visit our church if they do not have one and feel a need. In this witness there must be no manipulation or pressure.

Clinton Marsh, the first African American moderator of the PC(USA), wrote a book titled *Evangelism Is. . . .* In his chapter "Faith in Action," he speaks of an evangelistic ministry to prisoners and offers wisdom: "The hand and word of friendship must not be manipulative. To capitalize on misery, distress, and fear in order to maneuver someone into 'accepting Christ' is unchristian and may trigger a reactive rejection, not only of the 'decision,' but [also] of the church itself. Again, the key is to offer love and the truth and the opportunity to let Christ correct their lives in the most sensitive, nondirective manner. Jesus would claim their souls."[21]

Another example: although we may be committed to the cause of fair wages for all, we also belong to a community of faith, hope, and love. Our sense of justice begins with the salaries we pay all members of the church staff. We do not view people merely as wage earners or employees, but especially as human beings with material and existential needs.

Mission can lead to social and political revolution, but the reason behind our defense of those whose basic human rights are violated is the Lord of Life, not a transitive ideology. The Sermon on the Mount, especially the version in Luke 6, and Mary's Song in Luke 1:46–55 were revolutionary in that day and even now. Yes, we may fight, protest, and advocate for the rights of others and against abusive practices, but we do it in the name and in the spirit of Jesus Christ. In my conversations with Presbyterians who are adamant social activists, I am distressed when they say, "I can't tolerate those who have an evangelism fixation." Likewise, I am sad when someone excited about personal or international evangelism snidely remarks, "Those activists are too political for me." When we see mission as holistic, we are happy to have others do what is hard for us to do. We see what we do as only a part of the puzzle, as incomplete.

4. *The World Council of Churches (WCC) affirms, "There is no evangelism without solidarity; there is no Christian solidarity that does not involve sharing the knowledge of the kingdom which is God's promise to the poor of the earth."* Not many Presbyterians in the United States are comfortable with both of the words "evangelism" and "solidarity." For Christians in the Southern hemisphere, they go together quite naturally. The WCC's statement goes on to affirm: "There is here a double credibility test: A proclamation that does not hold forth the promises of the justice of the kingdom to the poor of the earth is a caricature of the Gospel; but Christian participation in the struggles for justice which does not point towards the promises of the kingdom also makes a caricature of a Christian understanding of justice."[22]

So could much of what we do and say with good intentions in our mission outreach simply be "a caricature of the Gospel"? Could our bumper stickers, mobilization, and efforts be "a caricature of a Christian understanding of justice"? Ouch! This hurts. It sounds as though the credibility of all we do depends on our commitment to the holistic nature of God's mission. Seeing only part of the picture is worse than counterproductive. A lot is at stake.

5. *The gospel mandate is not to increase church membership rolls, but to invite all people to become authentic disciples of Christ.* Evangelism is making disciples (Matt. 28:19–20). All of us are disciples who are constantly learning. At the same time we seek to invite and disciple others. Authentic and costly discipleship results in an empathetic awareness of the sufferings and injustices of people and creation and an incarnational insertion into the lives of those who suffer. Disciples of Jesus feel and experience the pain our Lord felt when he saw the suffering of the blind, the lame, the women, and the children who were rejected. Disciples weep as Jesus wept over the city of Jerusalem and at the death of Lazarus. Disciples feel anger over injustices as Jesus did when he saw people being exploited in the temple. When we take on the pain of others as Jesus did in his incarnate body, this leads to ministries of compassion and justice.

The Both/And Path

What does embracing the big picture of God's mission entail? What are some of the paradoxes involved in integration and convergence? First, we must understand that *Christians both* cooperate *ecumenically and* compete *evangelistically with others.* Let me explain what I mean because I generally reject competition. Christians, churches, religions, governmental and non-governmental agencies all need to cooperate in seeking sustainable solutions to the global food crisis, the HIV/AIDS pandemic, and the ecological crisis in order to promote fullness of human life on the planet. We do this with no intention of proselytism. In other words, as we engage in these efforts together, we do not try to pressure or manipulate others to join our faith community. At the same time, we do seek opportunities and respectful ways to share our faith in Christ with others. In this sense, we are competing fairly with other religious faiths that also evangelize.

Another way of saying this is that we practice both *dialogue* and *witness* with people of other faiths. Christians *witness* to persons of other religions and to secular persons with no religious affiliation through our lifestyle and faith sharing when we discern it is appropriate. In our conflicted and multi-religious world, we have no choice but to learn to dialogue with persons of other faiths. Dialogue permits a creative tension between interfaith cooperation and witness. In authentic dialogue, Bosch says, there is mutual learning while "asserting both ultimate commitment to one's own religion and genuine openness to another's."[23] This kind of dialogue is not a threat to our faith or a compromise of it. On the contrary, such dialogue can strengthen our faith and demonstrate the fruit of the Spirit. Respect for other people's consciences *is itself* a Christian witness because it shows that we believe humans are made in God's image and must be treated accordingly. To be credible today, our Christian witness must be *both* dialogical *and* collaborative.

While many African Christians are suffering from violence caused by tensions between Muslims and Christians in their countries, hosts of Christians in Africa live side by side in harmony with their Muslim neighbors. They collaborate in community efforts to engender peace, food security, sustainable agriculture, health care, and quality education for all. At times they respectfully share their religious commitment with one another. My African friends tell me that the two points where their witness strikes a real chord is when they share who Jesus is to them and the great power of God's Spirit over all other spirits. As a result, many Muslims have become followers of Jesus.

Second, in order to engage in holistic mission, we need to be *both evangelistic and ecumenical.* When we practice evangelism, we often invite people to join our particular faith community. Desiring the numerical growth of our congregation is certainly at issue. It is good to attract new members. Growth is healthy when it is holistic. We also want growth in discipleship and mission. However, sometimes for diverse reasons it is better to suggest that people with whom we share the gospel become a part of another church of their choosing.

We need to continually remember that we are building up the one universal church of Christ in many particular communities and denominations. We desire the growth of all churches. We are not simply competing with others in the aggressive spirit of the market. Nor are we proselytizing or stealing sheep from other flocks. Sometimes one must stop to ask, "What is our motivation? Are we building up the body of Christ, or simply adding numbers to our own congregation?" We seek to evangelize the unchurched and secular agnostics. We receive seekers. Ecumenical evangelism is invitational, loving, gentle, and respectful of free choice.

Claire came to the water gymnastics class the first day on crutches and entered the water with some difficulty. "What happened?" her friend Janet asked. "I was hanging curtains and fell from a small ladder in my home. To complicate things, with the economic crisis, I had just been dismissed from my job. I am fighting with depression, but at least I want to lose the weight I gained while convalescing and get my muscle strength back." During the classes Janet, Claire, and Shirley conversed about everything. When Claire passed from a cane to just limping, Janet mentioned that she volunteered as a tutor in a computer class every Saturday afternoon in a Roman Catholic parish. Claire was interested in obtaining new marketable skills. Janet offered, "Would you like for me to give you a ride on Saturdays to the class?" Claire suspiciously responded, "You know I am not religious." Janet assured her that there were no strings attached. Claire took up the offer and started attending the classes.

One day Claire noticed a poster telling about the upcoming Easter Vigil. On the way home that day, she asked Janet about it. "That is my favorite service of the year. It captures the essence of the Christian faith with many symbols and much celebration. Shirley is going with me, and she is Presbyterian. Do you want to join us?" After some hesitation, Claire agreed. The three of them went.

It was a magnificent service with a celebration of Christ the light of the world, who was victorious over death; the cleansing and renewing waters of our baptism; and moving texts from the Word of God. Something deep inside of Claire was touched. For the first time she was ready to talk about God with her friends. Shirley shared some of the new ways of thinking about God she was learning from reading *The Shack*, and Claire asked to borrow the book.

As a result of more conversations with Janet and Shirley, Claire decided to get her life right with God, to become a disciple of Jesus Christ, and to begin attending a church. Over pizza one night, she expressed this desire to her two friends and told them that before her mother died, when she was a child, she attended an Assembly of God congregation with her, and that there was one near her home that always held some mysterious attraction. Janet and Shirley encouraged her to visit the congregation and to talk with the pastor. Soon she was an active member there. She had a new job in a computer company and was walking with only a slight limp. This is an example of holistic ecumenical evangelism.

⚜⚜⚜⚜⚜⚜⚜

Finally, we are called *both to* announce *the good news of Jesus Christ and to* denounce *the bad news—all the values, attitudes, structures, and actions in the world that are contrary to the realm of God.* Mission is both evangelical and prophetic. We follow the example of Jesus, who began his ministry "proclaiming the good news of God, and saying, 'The time is fulfilled, and the kingdom of God has come near; repent, and believe in the good news'" (Mark 1:14–15). We joyfully announce the presence of God's realm of love on earth here and now. We lovingly invite people to respond and to receive God's forgiveness and grace. The good news is that God is with us both in good times and bad times. God knows and loves us and cares about our daily lives and problems. In holistic mission, we do everything we can to make known the good news. But that is only one side of the coin.

Jesus also is our model in confronting every part of our own lives and institutions that is not in accord with the values of God's realm. This is hard because we usually are blind to our own attitudes and incoherences. Often we pray the prayer of repentance in church without really owning it personally. On Monday morning we are back to the same sins. The prophetic denunciation of greed, pride, self-sufficiency, superiority, cheating, violence, discrimination, and economic exploitation begins with us and our own Christian community and our society. Courageously, we must confront the unjust and unfair structures that bring benefits to some and cause much harm to others. It took years for some churches to recognize, repent of, denounce, and seek reparation for the sinfulness of slavery, the Holocaust, and apartheid. We continually seek to empower people in order to transform the structures that perpetuate the bad news.

Integrating Many Parts into One Mission

Integrating the many parts in which we and many others participate into the holistic mission action of the triune God is complex. It requires that we keep before us the big picture of God's plan for the whole of creation. We have to believe that God's mission sends the church into the world to engage in three distinct interwoven, but not disconnected, missional activities: evangelism, compassionate service, and social justice. We have to open ourselves to understanding many ways of engaging in mission, some of which we have never even considered to be mission.

Integration and convergence are difficult because we tend to focus attention on the parts. Often we lift up one aspect and criticize the others. To integrate the parts, we have to be committed more to fullness and wholeness of faith than to our own agenda or preference. When we decide to see each component of mission as a vital part of the whole and in relation to the other parts, we get out of our comfort zone. When we choose to value differences rather than defend our priorities, we make ourselves vulnerable. When we take seriously the challenge to find convergence, it is unsettling because suddenly the boundaries become fuzzy. Over time, we can celebrate together the unity and diversity in God's mission and integrate our own mission practices into the whole. A missionary dialogue between those who engage in evangelism, compassionate service, and social justice is as hard as juggling three balls without dropping one. It will take a lot of coordination and patience.

Are you willing and ready to work on mission convergence?

Chapter 2

Who Is Engaged in Mission Today?

Many Participants in God's Mission: Expanding Partnerships

Around the dinner table at a Presbyterian Church (U.S.A.) mission conference, someone commented that networks are one of the newest and most exciting developments in mission today. A person asked, "Can you give me an example?"

The coordinator of the Presbyterian Hunger Program enthusiastically answered: "An example of collaboration between Christians in the North and in the South is the international Joining Hands[1] initiative. The JH builds bridges of solidarity between PC(USA) congregations and presbyteries and networks overseas. Most of us think of networks based in the United States and existing between groups in the states. In this case, PC(USA) presbyteries link up with autonomous networks in other countries composed of churches, grassroots community groups, and nongovernmental organizations (NGOs). Together they fight against the root causes of hunger and search for alternative economic activities that promote human dignity and self-sufficiency."

Another person inquired: "Do we have a network in Peru?"

"Yes, and it is an inspiring model," the coordinator continued. "Joining Hands–Peru (JH-Peru) promotes participatory processes in search of holistic and sustainable human development. It seeks the empowerment of civil society to improve the quality of life of all in Peru."

The whole table was following the discussion. Someone asked: "Who participates?" The coordinator explained: "Of the twenty Peruvian members in the network, four are churches, two are community-based groups, and nine are NGOs. The participation of the Roman Catholic Church alongside several Protestant denominations is an example of mission solidarity." A young person asked: "Who are the PC(USA) participants?" "The Presbytery of Giddings Lovejoy is the PC(USA) partner with the network. PC(USA) mission personnel serve as Companionship Facilitators."

A person who had not yet contributed spoke up. "I know of a congregation that has visited a church in the town of Moyobamba, Peru. Is that connected with the JH network?" Someone said, "There is the Peru Mission Network. Are they the same?" The PC(USA) regional liaison for South America spoke up. "We have a dynamic Peru Mission Network. Several congregations with connections in Moyobamba are involved. Some of them do medical work with the Luke Society."

"So is it a Moyobamba network?" "No," the liaison quickly replied; "there are also some congregations who started working in Iquitos and on the river. That had some problems. Now the Outreach Foundation, a Validated Mission Support Group of the PC(USA) committed to international programs of evangelism, is also supporting new work in the south in Arequipa. Others are working with a presbytery and congregations in Lima and others in the Andean region."

Someone observed, "It sounds like a PC(USA) invasion of Peru. Who are the Peruvian partners?" "Important question," the liaison said. "The first work in Iquitos started that way. The Evangelical Presbyterian and Reformed Church in Peru (IEPRP) expressed concern. Our area coordinator assured them that Presbyterians do mission in partnership. Conversations and visits started between our two denominations. As a result, we have recently signed a formal partnership agreement with the Evangelical Presbyterian and Reformed Church in Peru. We also are developing a relationship with an older and larger denomination with a strong Reformed heritage, the Evangelical Church of Peru (IEP)."

"So how did the network start?" She continued, "The staff in Louisville invited all of the congregations involved in Peru and representatives from the IEPRP to come together to form a network. The moderator of the IEPRP made a presentation of the missiological vision, work, needs, and strategies in the whole country. He described three hub cities strategic for programs of new church development."

The person whose question was left hanging asked: "Is the JH network a part of the Peru Mission Network or completely separate from it?" The liaison replied, "Congregations working with JH have participated in the network meetings."

The meal was over. As people got up to rush off to the meeting, someone made a final comment, "In mission today, there sure are lots of players on the field!"

⸙⸙⸙⸙⸙⸙⸙

How are all the players connected? How do we expand our partnerships? Why is it important for groups within the PC(USA) to do mission together? Can mission promote unity and overcome competition in the PC(USA)? How can Presbyterian Frontier Fellowship, Presbyterian Global Fellowship, and Presbyterian Peace Fellowship[2] join hands as partners in mission? Why is it sometimes easier for us to work with our global partners than with each other in our own ecclesial body? What is our changing role in the greater global church? How do we become more ecumenical?

Continuity and Historic Commitments

Why do we continue to do mission in partnership? Not merely because it has been a slogan in ecumenical church councils for nearly a century. Not because it is popular for business in a globalized world. Not for pragmatic or strategic reasons. Not because our practice is perfect. Presbyterians do mission in partnership for biblical and theological reasons. We do mission in partnership because of our missiology. What do we believe about God's mission in the world? I wrote the following in another book:

> The Trinity is a community of mutuality and reciprocity that reaches out beyond God's self to create and love the world. . . . Partnership is not merely a means, method, or approach to mission. *Partnership is a fundamental dynamic of the triune missionary God of love who is, acts, and relates in mutual partnership in sending the Son, the Spirit, and the church into the world as instruments of God's saving mission.*[3]

Now, this is serious stuff. Can we possibly be included in the triune missionary action and dialogue? Are we coactors with God? This is exactly what the Bible teaches. As José Míguez Bonino says, God's mission "enables, demands, and incorporates the 'partner' God has chosen into its own dynamic."[4] God invites us into the Trinitarian love, unity, and mission partnership. Theologian Shirley C. Guthrie says that as "junior"[5] partners of the triune God, we become partners of one another in God's mission. What a privilege and responsibility!

The policy statement "Presbyterians Do Mission in Partnership" says: "The discipline of partnership" recognizes "our human limitations" and "our fundamental unity in Jesus Christ" and "broadens our awareness of how interconnected God's mission is at the local, national, and global levels." Furthermore, "The practice of partnership guides our whole connectional church," meaning both "within and beyond our connectional community." Partnership means "that mission can best be done by joining hands with those who share a common vision. Partnership in mission involves two or more organizations who agree to submit themselves to a common task or goal, mutually giving and receiving and surrounded by prayer."[6]

Churches have been talking about mission in partnership for eighty years.[7] However, our practice is still in its beginnings. Partnership is a discipline that takes much endurance, patience, dialogue, learning, and unlearning. I have been a part of conversations with our partner churches in South America. I have also witnessed numerous groups coming to the South to do work projects. As I observe them interact and give, I see how difficult it is to have a truly equal relationship. We have a hard time letting go of control and coming with "empty hands." Our tendency is to take the initiative. Following or waiting for others is not easy. We are learning to go slowly and share experiences, projects, resources, and responsibilities.

When PC(USA) congregations make contact with some person or congregation in Peru or any other country, they should inquire to see if it is a partner church of the denomination. An example might be the large Presbyterian Church of Brazil. In 1859 it was founded by a precursor of the PC(USA) and was our partner until breaking unilaterally with us at our reunion in 1983. Since then the PC(USA) has developed partnerships with two other Presbyterian denominations in Brazil. One of them is the Independent Presbyterian Church of Brazil (IPIB). Its national mission agency launched a bold church-planting initiative called Sertão I in the arid Northeast region of Brazil. With the guidance of the Outreach Foundation and mission personnel, many PC(USA) congregations became involved in this project. Now the initial church plants have been turned over to the IPIB presbytery. The national leadership first asked PC(USA) congregations to channel all their support through the national offices and to inform them of all visits. Later they said it was time to end their support and leave it to the local presbytery. Now Sertão II has started in three more cities. Some PC(USA) congregations are participating in it. However, the Brazilian missionaries are the initiators and leaders. They organized the Vacation Project 2009, in which groups of young people from other regions of Brazil spent their summer vacations working with the lay Brazilian missionaries. As a result, new people started participating in the life of the congregations. The project included a small music school for children and youth and peewee soccer, led by a Brazilian student intern from the Center for Missionary Training in the city of Natal. Congregations need to understand our partners and respect their human and material resources and leadership.

In over 170 years of Presbyterian mission work, bilateral church-to-church relationships have been birthed, developed, and nurtured with 167 denominations in 80 countries. Those partnerships have gone through many stages, including moratoriums. Some of our partners in Africa and South Korea are larger than the PC(USA) and send their own mission workers to other countries. Together we do three-way mission in other more needy places and explore new mission challenges such as the HIV/AIDS epidemic and reconciliation. In most of our bilateral relationships, there has been a reversal of roles. They guide, lead, and challenge us. We learn to listen to and follow their advice.

In addition to the long-term bilateral church-to-church relationships, the PC(USA) participates actively in a web of ecumenical councils at global, continental, regional, and national levels. Today at these councils we sit side by side with many of our partner denominations, which challenge us with prophetic visionary action. The Middle East Council of Churches is a shining example that inspires and guides us. They gather Arab Presbyterian, Catholic, and Orthodox Christians who together have provided emergency assistance to refugees from Palestine and Iraq, offered solidarity to Arab Christians within Iraq, and sought to build peace in the region.

Under the umbrella of these bilateral and ecumenical relationships, there are 118 presbytery and synod international partnerships, and many local congregations have partnerships. Furthermore, PC(USA) mission work goes beyond these traditional relationships. Examples are the nine Joining Hands networks as well as multidenominational partnerships among "unreached" peoples. In a "twinning" program in Russia, congregations are matched with Orthodox, Baptist, or Lutheran congregations.

Partnership first of all means continuity and commitment to our bilateral and ecumenical relationships. We treasure these connections of quality and depth.

Changes in Global Mission Work

The Presbyterian Church (U.S.A.) values and builds on 170 years of developing church-to-church relationships as well as our participation in ecumenical councils. In response to the constant requests from partners, Presbyterian World Mission continues to send mission workers to meet the specific needs that our partners define. But we must also move beyond traditional patterns. We must embrace the commitment to change the way we do mission. This is the hard part because it takes us out of our comfort zones. Mission gets messy. What is changing is not the challenge to engage in God's holistic mission, but the fullness and complexity of participants. More individuals and local congregations are directly involved in global mission experiences and partnerships. More groups of mission initiators are being formed within the denomination. All of them are finding more new partners. The way all of these mission participants relate to each other and to the denominational agency, Presbyterian World Mission, is changing.

What are the greatest changes in mission? First and foremost, I see us moving *beyond one centralized mission-sending agency limited to bilateral partnerships and ecumenical councils.* As we organize ourselves for mission in the twenty-first century, we are experiencing tensions between the traditional centralized mission boards of denominations and the visionaries who are forming and leading multiple mission groups everywhere. This requires changes in our denominational structures of mission.

Dialogue, listening, and sharing are paramount as denominational agencies relate to many mission initiators today. Most people do not realize how many people in their denomination participate in God's mission. Change in structures requires genuine dialogue among all groups engaged in mission. We must learn to dialogue with each other about our understandings, relationships, past experiences, practices, and future possibilities in mission. And we must dialogue about issues of power and control. Centralized mission agencies no longer completely control denominational mission work around the world. We must humbly remember that it is God's mission and that God is in control. We learn to pray as Jesus did, "Not my will but yours be done" (Luke 22:42).

From the Trinity we discover that mission is a fellowship of many participants. Sometimes those of us in the Northern hemisphere concentrate on learning to listen and receive from our partners in the South and then forget to listen to each other. In this day of continuity and tremendous changes, "the PC(USA) has enormous possibilities to test out new ideas in practice as we enter more deeply into conversation with local congregations and judicatories as well as with churches and mission organizations both here and overseas."[8]

A second change is *decentralized mission.* To illustrate this massive change, Hunter Farrell, Director of Presbyterian World Mission, speculates that our centralized mission board is now doing perhaps only 10 percent of the global mission work of Presbyterians. This means that 90 percent has been decentralized. In other words, we are recognizing the role of all baptized Christians and local congregations. Our baptism is our commission to be disciples and mission workers. Whenever we serve God as lights and salt in the world, whether it is sharing the gospel with a friend, taking a plate of food to the hungry, advocating for fairness in global trade, or participating in a new mission partnership, we are a part of God's mission.

The congregation is now the primary locus of mission both locally and globally. This was the conclusion of an analysis of American Presbyterians done in the late 1980s by three scholars. A summary of the results is found in

Vital Signs: The Promise of Mainstream Protestantism. This change is called "the Organizational Revolution." The trend includes more "designated giving" and "localism—the desire to spend money on clearly identifiable causes at the local level." Coalter, Mulder, and Weeks affirm: "By the 1990s, the outline of the denominational revolution was clear. Congregations, rather than denominations, had become the primary mission organizations in American mainstream Protestantism."[9]

Local congregations reach out in their communities in evangelism and service. You join efforts with many local ecumenical groups to practice compassion and interreligious dialogue. Housing projects, services to the homeless, job training, soup kitchens, and advocacy on issues of social and economic justice unite people of many religious faiths in mission.

There is a growing mission mobilization, deployment, and engagement around the world. Many Presbyterians are involved directly in global mission today. More people are connected. There is more interface space and personal involvement. Global hands-on involvement has been facilitated by technology and ease in transportation. In an address to leaders of the Presbyterian Church (U.S.A.) mission networks, Robert Priest, professor of mission and intercultural studies at Trinity Evangelical Divinity School, said that short-term mission trips are "an enormous phenomenon" and "central to the ministry practices of a high proportion" of Christians in the United States. According to his research, it is likely that more than two million U.S. Christians travel abroad on short-term mission trips every year. Participation is particularly high among younger people.[10] As many local congregations and presbyteries develop long-term partnerships with congregations and presbyteries in other countries, a third change has occurred.

Being a connectional church, a third new idea we have tested is *networking.* Around ten years ago, the PC(USA) denominational mission agency invited congregations engaged in certain countries to come together a form a country mission network. The idea caught on. Today PC(USA) local congregations and judicatories with global partnerships have formed thirty-seven country networks from Cameroon to Central Asia to China to Cuba to Vietnam, Peru, Malawi, Russia, and others. There are also nongeographical groups, such as the Kurd Network, which is based on interest in a scattered people group, and a Water Network, which deals with this crucial global issue.

The World Mission Web site offers a definition for this phenomenon:

Mission Networks bring together Presbyterians from around the United States who share a common international mission focus. World Mission Networks facilitate building and maintaining healthy partnerships, and provide a place for representatives of various PC(USA) partnerships to share information and coordinate their efforts. Each Mission Network centers around a specific country, people group, or program area of ministry, and is composed of Presbyterians who represent international mission partnerships established trough their synods, presbyteries, congregations, or other PC(USA) entities.[11]

Another example is the Joining Hands networks of the Presbyterian Hunger Program mentioned in the case study at the beginning of this chapter. The history of the Presbyterian Hunger Program (PHP) is in itself an example of collaboration between the Northern and Southern streams of Presbyterians in the United States. They combined their hunger ministries in a joint program even before reunion in 1983. In 2000 the PHP launched a bold new initiative called Joining Hands Against Hunger (JHAH), which seeks to restore wholeness in God's creation and provide fullness of life for all. Later, the last two words were dropped and it became simply Joining Hands (JH). There are now nine country networks with partners in ten PC(USA) presbyteries. As South America Liaison for World Mission (whose job is all about connections and collaboration), I have seen the courageous beauty of the JH networks in Peru and Bolivia.[12]

A challenge I see now is the issue that surfaced in the case study. How can PC(USA) congregations and presbyteries in country networks and those in JH networks learn from one another in one network? The new mission statement of the Peru Mission Network adopted in 2009 shows the results of the road traveled since the early experiences in the case study:

> Under the Lordship of Jesus Christ, the Peru Mission Network is a group of Presbyterian (U.S.A.) churches, presbyteries, and individuals that fosters and coordinates mutual ministry in partnership, primarily with the Evangelical Presbyterian and Reformed Church of Peru (IEPRP), Biblical University of Latin America (UBL), Evangelical Church of Peru (IEP), and Joining Hands Network, and communicates with those involved in other mission efforts in Peru.[13]

The statement is found on the site that helps connect many mission participants under one umbrella of information. The site equips churches and organizations to better address mission in Peru and encourages sharing by mission personnel (including Young Adult Volunteers), partners in Peru, and mission teams. The use of Internet and information technology is a vital tool in mission connections today. One advantage of networking is that each group maintains autonomy as they engage in distinct parts of God's holistic mission.

According to the PC(USA) mission professor and former mission worker Stanley H. Skreslet, "networking" is a new model of mission whose institutional form is mirrored in the "nongovernmental organization" (NGO). It reflects the trend to "build relationships, expand alliances, and establish networks of groups and individuals committed to values implied by the biblical reign of God." In addition to being flexible and holistic, networking is *"essentially egalitarian.* It assumes no fixed center. Networks do not need hierarchies and function most purely without them. Networking is thus rigorously horizontal in approach, rather than vertical, and is founded on the ideal of interdependent relationships."[14] Let me give you an example.

I participated in the Brazil, Colombia, and Peru network meetings held after Mission Celebration 2007 in Louisville, Kentucky. There I saw the energy of the network approach as many PC(USA) networks scheduled their meetings simultaneously following that conference. The experience was so successful that it was repeated at Mission Celebration 2009 in Cincinnati. I also saw the challenges as on both occasions we were trying to start up a new Brazil network among congregations working with several different Presbyterian denominations in Brazil.

Later I participated in a follow-up meeting of network leaders with World Mission regional liaisons and staff in 2008 in Louisville. There were thirty networks participating. It was amazing to see how enthusiastically we learned from and resourced one another. We appointed an interim group to create a network-connections platform that would keep all networks informed about our various programs and facilitate communication with the Presbyterian Church (U.S.A.) at large. This interim committee proposed the selection of eight regional representatives from different networks to form a permanent communications coordinating committee. I am sold on this new model, which gathers together and integrates parts of the body who participate in God's mission in relationship to one another. The sum is indeed greater than the parts.

A fourth change, which is part of decentralizing and networking, is *multiple mission groups.* Another term for this might be mission initiators. Rob Weingartner calls them "Missions within the Mission." Simply put, in recent decades many groups of Presbyterians have organized "to focus passion and resources on mission in ways that [go] beyond the work of the denomination's mission offices."[15] There has been much cooperation and support of the centralized agency, but not without tensions.

In 1988 the General Assembly Council of the PC(USA) recognized Validated Mission Support Group status for three of these groups: the Medical Benevolence Foundation (MBF), the Outreach Foundation (TOF), and Presbyterian Frontier Fellowship (PFF). They entered into a covenant relationship with the General Assembly Council, which has resulted in mutual trust and support. Then going one step further in 2006, "TOF and PFF announced a strategic initiative to send more Presbyterians in mission service, through the PC(USA), through other agencies, and under their own appointment, all using a faith-mission approach to missionary support."[16] The result is one more mission group: the Antioch Partners (TAP). New tensions and challenges constantly present themselves as these groups seek to work respectfully together.

Multiple new mission groups have continued to emerge. Alongside the many partnerships and networks are diverse groups such as Presbyterian Global Fellowship and Presbyterian Peace Fellowship. Presbyterian Global Fellowship is a group that started in 2006 with less formal connection to the denomination. It is committed to renewal of the church around its missional purpose and encourages PC(USA) congregations to build new partnerships with the majority church in the Global South. For years Presbyterian Peace Fellowship has been training volunteers to be part of an accompaniment program in Colombia and other countries involved in struggles for building peace and justice. This is mission as advocacy for human rights. It is also in solidarity with those seeking an Israeli-Palestinian peace. The Association of Presbyterian Mission Pastors (APMP) was founded in 1989. It is a network of mission pastors and directors of local church mission in conversation with denominational leaders. Pittsburgh Theological Seminary formed World Mission Initiative, which has facilitated cross-cultural mission experiences for seminarians. Much of its engagement is in mission as frontier evangelism.

The fifth change comes full circle with *new roles and relationships in denominational centralized agencies.* Mission is at the heart of the General Assembly Council of the Presbyterian Church (U.S.A.). This became obvious in a recent restructuring. Holistic local-global mission is practiced especially in three ministry areas: Evangelism and Church Growth; Compassion, Peace, and Justice; and World Mission. The Compassion, Peace, and Justice unit coordinates several distinct programs: Presbyterian Disaster Assistance, Presbyterian Hunger Program, Presbyterian Peacemaking Program, Presbyterian Washington Office, and Self-Development of People. Those engaged in these programs partner with each other, with World Mission, and with others to enable a fullness of partnerships. The areas of Interfaith Relations and International Health Ministries in World Mission join in the cross-fertilization of holistic mission. Presbyterian Women are also very active in local and global mission. We are all challenged to work together in the fullness of mission.

The centralized agency Presbyterian World Mission (WM) continues to develop the rich mission heritage of enduring relationships with our global partners. There are more requests from our partners to send mission personnel than WM is able to send. The General Assembly has committed to increasing the number of full-time, compensated mission workers to 215 in 2009 and 220 in 2010. Additionally, Young Adult Volunteers are sent both internationally and in the United States. World Mission also continues to receive mission workers from our partner churches to serve in the United States in many capacities.

As a result of other changes mentioned above, the greatest innovation in WM is the new office on Equipping for Mission Involvement (EMI). In response to the proliferation of mission groups, partnerships, networks, and local congregations-in-mission, the centralized agency is challenged to equip the church for transforming mission. This equipping and resourcing role involves providing biblical materials on mission theology and practice, recommended reading, as well as materials on organization, stewardship, and direct involvement. It also includes providing the Mission Networks with several central ways of communicating among themselves and with World Mission. The EMI set up a PC(USA) "splash page"[17] and a Web-based "wisdom community," where networks and others may interact in a participatory process. The name is "Mission Crossroads PC(USA)."[18] Inside this community are subgroups or rooms, one for each Mission Network, as well as rooms for other mission initiators. This encourages cross-pollination among different mission-related groups. Additionally, EMI invited each presbytery to appoint a World Mission Advocate and organized a meeting to orient them.

World Mission is rising to the challenge and preparing written and electronic resources that help us answer many pressing questions and examine our practices and attitudes. How do we avoid perpetuating the mistakes of neocolonialism and neoimperialism? How do we think about and talk with people in other cultures and religions? How do we organize networks? How do we form new partnerships with discernment? Staff is providing training events at all levels.

The consultant role of World Mission's area coordinators, regional liaisons, and mission personnel assigned as partnership facilitators and delegation hosts is key in sharing information. They know the partners, histories, cultures, relationships, and programs. These are valuable human resources for coordination and connections. Furthermore, as missiologist Paul Pierson writes, they can provide guidance to avoid a poor use of resources, "exploitation of well-meaning Western Christians," or "paternalism and dependency. Here mission agencies are a great source of expertise, advice, and encouragement."[19]

Here we have identified five major changes: (1) beyond centralized mission-sending agency, (2) decentralized mission, (3) networking, (4) multiple mission groups, and (5) new roles in denominational agencies. In all of these changes, it becomes obvious that it is better for us to work together in God's mission. We are learning to move beyond individual mission initiatives. Today networks, partnerships, team efforts, and strategic collaboration of mission organizations focus on interdependence and informal relationships. Specialized mission organizations and new initiatives supplement, support, and serve churches and denominational agencies. They strengthen bilateral partnerships and give rise to new forms of engagement beyond present partnerships. Pierson points us to the need for more cooperation with "multidenominational and multinational partnerships" and encourages us to relate to the "new, cutting-edge movements in the majority world, both to learn from them and to discover how we can serve the *missio Dei* together."[20]

With the increase of multiple mission initiators and "mission-sending" groups, today there is a need for formal or informal structures of connectedness[21] that facilitate missiological dialogue, mutual accountability, and a common agreement on the guiding principles of a unified witness to the world.[22] Each group represented in these five changes can share its unique gifts, commit to build bridges, and see its mission structures as part of the whole church and of the mystery of God's holistic mission.

Connections and Convergences

In all that we have discussed, it is obvious that we need to move beyond our tendency to be Lone Rangers in mission. We must face and overcome our animosity, fear, competition, and disagreements. Some problems we face when we are not connected in mission are fragmentation, isolation, and probably irrelevance. The involvement of individuals and congregations in mission is good as long as our participation fits into the big picture. We are better together with many other participants. Let me share with you three major events that represent a new moment of connections and convergence in the worldwide mission web.

1. Global Christian Forum: A Broader Ecumenism

The Global Christian Forum held near Nairobi, Kenya, November 6–9, 2007, is paradigmatic of structural changes in mission partnerships today. Recognizing that the ecumenical movement is broader than the World Council of Churches, a Forum was proposed. The WCC initiated the nine-year process and defined itself as "one of the participating organizations alongside others."

With 240 representatives from Protestant, Anglican, Orthodox, Catholic, Evangelical, and Pentecostal churches and interchurch organizations from over 70 countries, it was the "most diverse Christian gathering ever to discuss unity and common witness."[23] Samuel Kobia, WCC General Secretary, said at the opening: "I hope that we will take the risk of working together" and forge "new relations among ourselves and between our churches" to strengthen Christian unity.[24]

The Final Message of the Nairobi Forum was a "historic breakthrough." The Global Christian Forum process will go forward as an open platform for encounter and dialogue. The goal is to "foster mutual respect, explore and address common challenges."[25] Participants affirmed their desire "to move out of the familiar ground, [and] to meet each other on a common ground where mutual trust might flourish," and where they "might be empowered to celebrate, enter into dialogue and act together" in spite of differences. The Final Message affirms the participants' commitment to promote "even greater understanding and cooperation among Christians" and to overcome divisions.[26]

A "Proposals for the Future" document clarified the Forum's focus on "relationships" and "conversations." Also, "any resulting joint actions will be outworked through the participating churches and organizations." The process will continue to be based on "committed participation" rather than become a "membership organization," and the "circle of participation" will be "broadened and deepened."[27]

This new ecumenical paradigm that brings more conversation partners to the table and moves beyond structures of formal membership can guide all ecclesial bodies as we mobilize a growing circle of participants in our mission endeavors. The voices of evangelicals and Pentecostals who have not earlier participated in the WCC help to keep the uniqueness of Christ and the call to make disciples from all peoples on the agenda.

2. Dallas Consultation: Invitation to Expanding Partnerships

The second moment of convergence was in Dallas, Texas, January 16–18, 2008. It was a PC(USA) Consultation on the Worldwide Mission of the Church titled "Renewed Call to Presbyterian Mission in the World: A Dialogue for Our Shared Future." The sixty-four participants, including many groups of mission initiators, represented the most diverse group of Presbyterians I have ever seen talking about core values and practices in mission. Leaders from World Mission and the three Validated Mission Support Groups were present. Others included representatives from Presbyterian Global Fellowship, Presbyterian Peace Fellowship, the Witherspoon Society, the PC(USA)-related mission networks, mission personnel, mission professors, Presbyterian Women, and global partners, including Vietnam, India, Colombia, Peru, Ghana, and others.

The final two-page document was an amazing consensus: "An Invitation to Expanding Partnership in God's Mission"[28] was signed by all participants. "We acknowledge the rich Presbyterian heritage in world mission and reaffirm the Presbyterian understanding of God's mission as it is expressed in *Gathering for God's Future*,"[29] it begins. The introduction then states:

> Grounded in this theological foundation we realize that God is calling us to new patterns of mission. The world has changed, and the majority of the world's Christians are now in Latin America, Africa and Asia. The great growth and mission faithfulness of the Church outside the West invite us into a new posture. We must listen and learn to receive. We must also be open to new patterns of collaboration. These new patterns involve new cooperation and partnerships within the PC(USA).

The document goes on to articulate the core values of trust, humility, holistic mission, complementary gifts, speaking and hearing the truth in love, sensitivity to contexts of massive global inequalities and issues of power, and long-term commitments. The value statements show that God's mission has many parts, many people, and many places.

It concludes with concrete ways the group will continue to "work cooperatively." Future tasks to propel the "Invitation to Expanding Partnership" movement forward were set forth: formation of a coordinating committee, collaboration in sending of mission personnel and expanding Presbyterian funding for mission personnel, and sharing this document with their constituencies.

The momentum of this mutual invitation to a common table, baptism, mission, and purpose was felt at the PC(USA) General Assembly in June 2008, which endorsed it. As of early 2009, some 66 groups had signed the document, including over 100 individuals and more than 20 congregations, presbyteries, and other organizations. The Coordinating Committee has met many times, and organized a working group at the Mission Celebration '09 to recommend more concrete steps for moving forward.

3. The Uniting General Council of the World Communion of Reformed Churches

The first moment of convergence was initiated by the World Council of Churches. The second encouraged internal mission connections within the Presbyterian Church (U.S.A.). The final convergence is the merging of two bodies—the World Alliance of Reformed Churches (WARC) and the Reformed Ecumenical Council (REC). The Uniting General Council will take place June 18–25, 2010, in Grand Rapids, Michigan. At that historic meeting, the two bodies will gather to formalize their merger to become the World Communion of Reformed Churches (WCRC). The Uniting General Council has a Web site that focuses on the activities that will occur during and after the creation of the new Reformed Church body, which will represent some 75 million Christians around the world.[30]

The new Reformed organization is defined by two core callings: the call to be a communion and the call to covenant for justice. The theme selected for the Council in 2010 reflects both calls. It comes from Ephesians 4: "Unity of the Spirit in the Bond of Peace."[31] The two key words in the theme, "unity" and "peace," must be held in balance as the two organizations become a new communion. The diversity of the churches and networks in both organizations is rich. There will be many benefits in the merger, as well as risks. It is a bold step and comes as the result of a long process of openness, patience, mutual respect, and dialogue.

It is appropriate and intentional that the World Communion of Reformed Churches comes into being in 2010. This is the centennial celebration of the first great ecumenical missionary conference in Edinburgh in 1910. It is a moment to remember that it was God's one mission that birthed the modern ecumenical movement.

Criteria for New and Old Partnerships with Integrity

By what criteria are our partnerships defined? The five Principles of Partnership in "Presbyterians Do Mission in Partnership" are excellent guides:

- Shared grace and thanksgiving
- Mutuality and interdependence
- Recognition and respect
- Open dialogue and transparency
- Sharing of resources

I also find helpful a statement from the Christian Conference of Asia of "approaches to mission that are rejected," as well as Guidelines for Sharing from the Consultation on Koinonia in El Escorial, and Basic Principles from the United Church of Christ in the Philippines.[32] Using these to orient us, I suggest the following criteria to guide the mission participants of the PC(USA) and others in defining new and old partnerships with integrity. I believe this is the way to intentionally overcome the Western neoimperialism of the twentieth century and truly practice partnership in the twenty-first century.

1. *Partnerships* are just and caring relationships between churches or organizations that share common callings and concerns. They agree to collaborate in the *missio Dei*, which promotes the reign of God. They engage in mission together from the perspective of a clear postcolonial, anti-imperialistic, anti-paternalistic missiology. Their different approaches, viewpoints, and practices are congruent with this perspective.

2. *Partnerships* are always two-way or multilateral relationships of reciprocity with shared decision making, open dialogue, and transparency concerning joint projects, strategies, funds, and mission personnel. This requires honesty and building trust. One-way relationships with initiative, domination, decisions, or control by one party are not partnerships. Unilateral relationships that do not ensure the dignity of others as subjects created in God's image are not partnerships.

3. In relationships with new global *partners*, the partner from the PC(USA) always enters at the invitation of others and never as leaders. In the missionary movement today, this shows true recognition and respect for the leadership of the global church in the South. It requires humility, dialogue, patience, and discernment.

4. *Partnership* calls for the mutual sharing of all types of resources, for mutual giving and receiving, for mutual service. Authentic partnerships begin with a long period of getting to know one another by sharing common experiences of faith and life. This means lots of face-to-face time together without agendas. Relationships based on money, one-way giving, or donor control are not true partnerships.[33]

5. *Partnership* calls for interdependence, in which mutual aid comes to all and where mutual circles of accountability reside. All monetary gifts of personal support to individuals should be avoided, with gifts always going through local accountability structures for the benefit of the whole community. All mission initiators and agencies should openly share what they give with other collaborators.

6. *Partnership* promotes respect for all historic PC(USA) partners and mutual cooperation between all PC(USA) participants in God's mission. We reject mission initiatives that might cause divisions, barriers, conflicts, rivalries, and competition in the one body of Christ.

7. *Partnerships* recognize that the church in each place has primary responsibility for evangelism in that place and the right to discern what the Spirit is doing in their midst. The indigenous church sets its own agenda. Partners from other places seek to discern the agenda of the national partner church

and to join them in it when invited. In prophetic actions, partners stand in solidarity and in advocacy on behalf of their partners. Only in certain special cases where there is no active indigenous church do partners from outside take initiatives in evangelism.

8. *Partnerships* fit within a greater picture of God's holistic local-global mission, with a rich fullness of participants in it. The partners seek to recognize and value all who are engaged in specific ministries, thus avoiding duplication of efforts and wastefulness and being responsible stewards of resources.

9. *Partnerships* can be nurtured by short-term mission trips and the service of short-term mission volunteers. However, they also value the need for long-term commitments to sustainability, integrity of creation, self-development, and self-support. They often require long-term mission personnel for guidance concerning culture, language, history, and relationships with partner churches. Mission means perseverance, endurance, and persistence. It is a dialogue where we have the freedom to say no and the discernment to hear and accept the no of our partners. In this dialogue it is also occasionally possible for one partner to say yes to something to which the other has not yet committed, such as evangelism of a nearby group.

10. *Partnerships* vary according to the objectives or kind of mission activity. In evangelism we support the efforts and leaders of national indigenous churches when present. In frontier evangelism, where there is no church, we respectfully join hands with neighboring churches and movements when possible or strike out on our own if necessary. In compassionate service and social justice, a broad array of partners is possible, including NGOs, networks, and councils.

11. As we seek to practice authentic *partnerships* with each other internally and with others around the world, six important keys are these: connectedness, cooperation, complementarity, communication, convergence, and consultation.

Critique and Tough Challenges

While we have discussed how many participants are involved today in the fullness of God's mission, do not be misled into thinking that all is well. The fact is, missiologist Philip Wickeri says, most people "too easily and uncritically" use the term "partnership." Wickeri helps us understand that "we are not there yet." We try to be partners. We do not want to be imperialists. Therefore, it is time to admit where our practice has fallen short. In other words, we need to be honest about the mistakes we make even when our intentions are good.

It is painful. We would rather pretend that all our partnerships are healthy. However, Wickeri gives us a reality check: "Without a critical perspective on existing mission practices, structures, and working styles, any statement on partnership in mission lacks a prophetic cutting edge."[34]

With so many players on the team, so many mission groups and initiators, so many local congregations, a lack of coordination and mixed missiologies can result in tensions. Sometimes in our enthusiasm and overpersonalization of mission, partner churches are ignored. Other times they are overstretched. Duplications occur. The same church is painted three times in one year. Many problems arise from a lack of training.

Good people make so many mistakes in mission. They include arrogance of thinking we know it all, discrimination, and a money-centered approach to mission. We often show insensitive and disrespectful attitudes without ever realizing it. Our political, economic, and cultural imposition influences our mission. Unfortunately, the tragedy of 9/11 and the war in Iraq have resulted in a new American assertiveness in the world. Perhaps, the economic crisis on the world agenda in 2009 will usher in a new era of global dialogue, collaboration, and solidarity.

A major obstacle in mission today is the spirit of competition between Christians and churches. For example, in 2007 I attended the First Ecumenical Missionary Congress of the National Council of Christian Churches of Brazil (CONIC). A recurring concern was the entrepreneurial spirit of the globalized free market. The result is mission and evangelism marked by rugged *competition* rather than by partnership. We must be critically aware of ways we fall into this competitive trap, both in our finances and in mission.

Our partner churches, often impatient with persistent inequalities, can help us understand where we, as Wickeri says, "have not been willing to follow through with the radical demands of what partnership and working together in God's mission requires."[35] For example, churches in the North often visit churches in the South and develop an ongoing relationship. They feel that they are in collaborative and reciprocal partnerships in mission. However, from the perspective of the "partners" in the South, the experience is one of Northern domination. The gringos are always in control of the "shared" projects. If we have a true relationship of trust with our partners, we must ask them to give us the critique we need to hear. I saw this happen in a U.S.A.-Brazil presbytery partnership. The Brazilian presbytery was so upset that it ended the partnership and wrote a letter detailing all its complaints. The leader of the presbytery in the North received it with respect and humility, wrote a letter of sincere apology and repentance, and an eventual dialogue over guidelines for partnerships restored the relationship.

Most of our difficulties go back to the issues of unequal power and money. We all resist this. Latin American missiologist Segundo Galilea says there are two models of mission: out of affluence and out of poverty.[36] The second is the New Testament model (2 Cor. 8:2–3) and is the model of the mission movement in the Global South today. Cuban churches are one good example. Every congregation of the Presbyterian-Reformed Church in Cuba has a ministry with seniors.

Probably the biggest area in which we have difficulty in receiving and understanding critique is the financial. I recently heard a speaker say that the average cost per person for a two-week mission trip to Peru is U.S. $1,800. That is the annual salary of most Peruvian pastors. What are some negative consequences of mission "out of affluence"?[37] As a result of social disparity between the North and South, true reciprocity and *interdependence* are difficult. Our giving can affect internal relationships of the partner churches we seek to help. For instance, when certain individuals or churches receive large gifts, the result can be envy and hostile relationships with others. Too much money too quick in a partnership can cause profound problems.

We cannot move into the new century and be talking about our partnerships without a critical reflection on unequal power and money. This issue is unavoidable. We must grapple with our affluence. How do we do mission together when material resources are so unevenly owned? Simpler lifestyles, work-styles, strategies, and administrative overhead might give us more credibility. We must also open ourselves to new patterns of mission. We can learn from the models in the New Testament and in the Global South. We must examine our patterns of giving and receiving. We need to recognize the fact that giving or spending sometimes can be harmful.[38]

The thesis of this chapter is straightforward. It is better to do mission together. What is at stake? Andrew Kirk states it clearly: "Failure of different Churches, agencies and individual Christians to work together wherever they can has a detrimental effect on mission. It causes a credibility gap between reality and the message [and] a tragic waste of resources in the duplication of time, money and human abilities."[39]

We face an abundance of complexities and tough challenges in doing God's mission collaboratively. Hunter Farrell reminds us, "A very uncertain economic future means that our mission work, like Christian discipleship, is not for the faint-hearted."[40] Demonstrating our unity and celebrating our diversity requires courage and patience. Mission together can be difficult, but under the lordship of Jesus Christ and the leadership of the Holy Spirit, it is possible. Jesus paid the price and gave the example:

Though he was in the form of God,
    did not regard equality with God
    as something to be exploited,
but emptied himself,
    taking the form of a slave,
    being born in human likeness.
And being found in human form,
    he humbled himself
    and became obedient to the point of death—
    even death on a cross.

(Phil. 2:6–8)

Remember always that the ultimate answer to the question "Who is engaged in mission today?" is GOD! *Missio Dei* is God's mission. We are invited to join the triune God, who is gathering together all the pieces of God's holistic mission and uniting all of the participants in the fullness of it. Jesus models partnership with the Father and Spirit and prays for Christians in mission "that they may all be one. As you, Father, are in me and I in you, may they also be in us, so that the world may believe that you have sent me" (John 17:21). Through our life in Christ and common witness, we become partners of the Lord of the church, who is filling and building up the PC(USA), the global faith community, and the universe, thus bringing in the realm of God for the glory of God.

Chapter 3

Where Is the Location of Mission Today?

Many Places in God's Mission: Local-Global Synergy

We usually think of the place of mission as either local or global. In the big picture, it might be both. I live in Curitiba, a lovely city of 1.8 million people in South Brazil. As PC(USA) regional liaison for South America, I have contacts with partner churches, mission personnel, ecumenical councils, and theological institutions throughout the continent. I also engage in missionary dialogue with World Mission staff in Louisville, Kentucky, and PC(USA) congregations through e-mails, visits, and conferences. Two of my colleagues have helped me see how particular churches organize and integrate their local-global mission endeavors.

The first opportunity came when Steve Earl invited me to be the speaker for the Preston Lecture Series at Shandon Presbyterian Church in Columbia, South Carolina. I selected the theme "God's Holistic Mission" and prepared a sermon based on Ephesians, a lecture on "The Integration of Evangelism, Compassionate Service, and Social Justice" and one on "Partnership in Local-Global Mission." From the beginning I sensed this congregation's mature understanding and deep commitment to holistic mission. I was as eager to learn from their experiences in mission as they were to learn from mine.

On Sunday, mission leaders gathered for a luncheon. They enthusiastically shared with me the vast range of commitments of their multiple mission teams. The Global Missions Team is involved in Honduras, Nicaragua, Sudan, Katrina relief work, and supports PC(USA) mission personnel and youth global missions. The Community Missions Team is active in a Women's Shelter, Family Shelter, Sister Care, Children's Chance, Salvation Army, migrant ministries, and youth local/national missions support. In addition, there is a Housing Team. Their concerns include affordable housing, Habitat for Humanity, homelessness and homeless shelters, and disaster response. The Hunger Team participates in the CROP Walk,

Meals on Wheels, Bread for the World, a soup kitchen, and Harvest Hope Food Bank.

Talk about holistic mission! I was impressed. There is more. The Health Team has an AIDS and Health Care Team and is involved in sexual trauma services, blood drives, and a counseling center. The Education Team works with the Presbyterian Student Association, Scouting, and Helping Hands in a middle school, alongside their engagement with educational issues and agencies in the community and state. The Peacemaking Team sponsors forums and conferences, practices environmental stewardship and church recycling, and participates in the state Christian Action Council. In addition to the teams, the congregation provides support through general per-capita funding, Unified Benevolences, Theological Education, New Kirk Church Development, Presbyterian Home Resident Aid, and support of a children's home.

After talking informally with the leaders of all these teams before and during lunch and answering their many questions after lunch, I reflected on the many parts and places of the mission engagement of Shandon Presbyterian Church. It was encouraging to see this church's mission commitment and leadership. It felt good to see folks doing global and local mission all together in harmony. Without a major reorganization plan that allowed members to participate in the teams of their choice, the congregation would probably still be going through the tedious process of recruiting members for traditional committees. It took bold initiative for the pastor to embark on this new way of organizing for mission. I experienced the fruits of the interactive structure. There was a missionary dialogue between those involved in local and global mission. For me the only missing piece was an Evangelism Team or its equivalent.

Another colleague who transformed the mission department of a local congregation is Art Beals. He shares this experience in his book *When the Saints Go Marching Out!* His congregation, University Presbyterian Church (UPC) in Seattle, Washington, also eliminated traditional committees and replaced them with small communities or task forces "tightly organized around very specific interests and program goals." The task forces are formed as members of the congregation answer the question, "What special mission concern invites my attention?"[1] Rather than recruiting people, they release people for ministries. The purpose of UPC's Department of Urban and Global Mission is "to plan and supervise the development and deployment of human, financial, and partnership resources for cross-cultural ministry opportunities locally, nationally, and globally."[2] Art further explains: "Our approach is comprehensive because we are committed to engage in mission at every appropriate level available to us: congregations, denomination, mission society, parachurch agency, national churches, and international mission structures."[3]

How do we relate local and global mission work in our globalized world? How do we organize our church mission structures for more synergy between activities at local, regional, national, and global levels? Where does local mission fit into the scheme of expanding ecumenical partnerships? Could reorganizing our work for a while eventually end up fragmenting mission further? What is it that really guides a congregation's many endeavors to authentic dialogue with each other across teams/committees/task groups? Could it be a dialogue pitched at a higher level of values and theology and practical learning about partnering? Are we eager and willing to work for such exchanges?

Local Congregations in Local Communities

The triune God of love is the source and initiator of all redemptive, healing, and reconciling actions in the universe. The location of God's missionary action is everywhere. Through baptism all Christians are called to become disciples-missionaries. Primary agents through whom God is doing mission today are the local congregation and the global church (see fig. 3.1).[4] God is working in mission in every place and is sending multiple mission participants and partners from everywhere to everywhere.

Who is the primary agent in God's mission in each local community? I remember participating in 1997 in the Congregations in Global Mission: New Models for a New Century Conference in St. Louis sponsored by the Presbyterian Church (U.S.A.). It was hailed by many as a "watershed event," and I feel that we are still living into the results of it. There was something new and something old at that conference. The new was that local congregations have assumed a new role as initiators and primary agents in global mission. In the conclusion of their extensive research project, Presbyterians Milton J. Coalter, John M. Mulder, and Louis B. Weeks affirmed that we have become a "new denomination" in which "the congregation is now the locus of power and mission."[5] It is the trend of localism or decentralization. The old was that local congregations have always been agents in local mission. In the opening plenary session, Clifton Kirkpatrick stated:

LOCAL-GLOBAL MISSION CHALLENGES
IN OUR WORLD

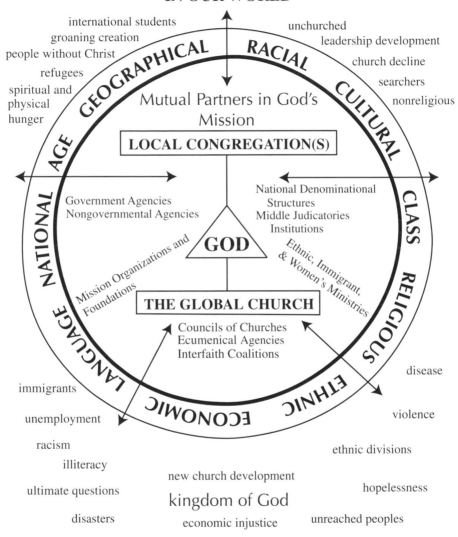

Fig. 3.1. Local-Global Mission Partners and Challenges

There is a renewed understanding that we are a missionary people and that each congregation is called to be in mission locally and globally. . . . In the past, international mission was done by the denomination for the churches. But, as we face a new century, what we know increasingly is that everything is local and everything is global and we've got to be working together to form new patterns of mission in the next century to . . . renew our congregations by our encounter with the global Christian community.[6]

Later Marian McClure challenged us to "bust" the local-versus-global dichotomy as well as other dichotomies that hinder our vision of the fullness or wholeness of God's mission.[7]

The cutting edge today is the *hyphen* in local-global mission. We don't know how to relate our local and global mission work! We struggle with the problem of place for Christian mission and the connection between global and local in our globalized world. How do we become truly mutual partners in local-global mission?

Where do we begin? Recognizing that God our Creator and Redeemer is at work in every space and place in the planet is the best way to begin. God's one holistic mission is both local and global. Every mission activity in every place is equally important in God's eyes. There is no second-class mission action. Keeping this big picture in mind helps us to place equal value on local and global mission. To some, global mission may seem more romantic, adventuresome, challenging, or exotic, but local community mission requires the same persistence and commitment. Often it is much more difficult and challenging. Sometimes it seems easier to relate to persons of other cultures in faraway places and for short times than to relate to those same cultures in our own neighborhoods. God calls the church to *both* local *and* global mission outreach.

Some congregations are stronger in their commitment and involvement in global mission while ignoring blatant needs in their own backyard. It is vital for them to seek new and innovative programs for mission in their local settings. Others are very active in local mission and community projects while ignoring crying pleas around the globe. It is important for them to become globally aware and to seek ways to support God's mission with others in distant places. In both cases, it is good to find your blind spots, to grow your weak links, to pursue the *both/and* path with the parts and places of mission.

With this in mind, I suggest that we look at the different locations of mission and then see how they fit together in synergy. Every local congregation in every place has the responsibility first to practice holistic mission in that place. We begin to do mission where we are. Every place is a mission field. No one understands a local community and culture better than those who live in it. Each local congregation is called to practice evangelism, compassionate service, and social justice in its own community and region. Furthermore, every baptized Christian is called to be a disciple and missionary. Every church member is a minister. The congregation is responsible to inspire members to discover their areas of interest and to discern God's call. It then empowers, equips, and organizes them to engage in mission in appropriate spheres. Every church everywhere is called to engage in local-global mission in cooperation with God's Spirit and with others in response to challenges and opportunities in its own context. Sometimes this means embarking on new missional experiments and new beginnings.

In being faithful to the church's primordial identity to proclaim and share the good news of the gospel of Jesus Christ, every congregation develops programs and practices of evangelism, new member recruitment, visitation, neighborhood Bible studies, and welcoming visitors. Whether you use the word "evangelism" or other terms, the important thing is sharing the message, inviting people to be disciples of Christ, nurturing them in the Christian faith, and equipping them for mission. Evangelism is an essential part of the mission of every local congregation.

Likewise, each local congregation is called to practice compassionate service. Jesus was aware of the many physical, emotional, social, and material needs of people all around him. He always responded to human need with compassionate acts. Therefore we must open our eyes to the pain and needs of those all around us. How many men, women, youth, and children in your immediate neighborhood and in your city are homeless, jobless, marginalized, abandoned, hungry, sick, lonely, or victims of violence? Is your congregation a healing community? There are opportunities and responsibilities for compassionate local mission service all around us. It is hypocritical to do building projects in other countries and ignore those without decent affordable housing in your own community.

Finally, each local congregation is called to practice social justice. We must consider the root and structural causes of suffering in our communities. Furthermore, corporate policies and actions of transnational companies in our local communities are sometimes responsible for suffering in communities around the world. Our ministries of social justice locally can have an impact globally. Why do some people have difficulty in acquiring jobs, homes, loans, health care, and education? What are the economic, educational, health, and social issues of people in your community and state? Where might the church engage in solidarity, advocacy, and political actions for change and justice? Jesus' mission included liberation of people from all kinds of oppression. What oppressions do people in your community suffer? Where can you come alongside them in their struggles? Is your congregation a part of the problem or a part of the solution? Is it a redemptive and liberating community?

My intention in this book is to help local congregations mobilize all their members in holistic mission practices both locally and globally. Mission begins at home yet never ends there. Our first challenge is to value all of the many pieces in the puzzle of God's local-global mission, to search for missing pieces in our geographical location, and to remember that we do mission better together. We know and make Christ known fully by doing mission more fully. Our local mission fits together into a bigger picture that is also global. Just as those who do evangelism, compassion, and justice need to engage in a missionary dialogue with one another, so do those who practice these activities locally and globally. Every local congregation everywhere is a primary agent in God's mission, but it is never a solitary agent. Dialogue! Dialogue! Dialogue! This is the way to convergence, synergy, and unity in God's one holistic mission.

Respecting Local Missiologies in Other Local Communities

In 1985 Robert J. Schreiter published the book *Constructing Local Theologies*. With local congregations existing in virtually every country in the world, he recognized their necessity of "making sense of the Christian message in local circumstances" and local cultures. He reminded us "that all theologies have contexts, interests, relationships of power, special concerns."[8] This was in line with the current missiological principle of contextualization. It is something we all practice in many ways without thinking about it. We do things in accord with our own environment, customs, history, education, and understanding. This is our context. We interpret what we hear and read in terms of the context that has nurtured us. We do many things unconsciously "the American way." We construct our theologies, liturgies, and missiologies in this framework.

The tricky part comes when we cross borders of any kind or distance and interact with local congregations in other contexts. The natural tendency of mission pioneers was to transplant and even impose their own understanding and language of theology and church on other local communities that had different worldviews, customs, and values. Finally, local congregations and theologians in Latin America, Africa, and Asia began saying in the 1970s, "Enough! We want to interpret Scripture, theology, church, and mission in terms that make sense in our own cultural context!" Asians insisted that Christianity will never take firm root and grow throughout Asia as long as it is a "Western religion." Africans declared that the "white man's Christianity" is often at odds with African theologians, does not use African instruments and dance in worship, and thus is unacceptable. Latin Americans insisted that a religion dominated by the rich will never liberate the oppressed poor. Women around the world began to read the Bible from the feminine perspective, to recover their dignity and ministry.

Since then, theologians on every continent have been doing theology, "doing" church, interpreting Scriptures, and practicing evangelism, compassion, and justice in ways that make sense in their context. They bring new questions and challenges to the global church. Just as we need one another to do mission fully, so we need one another in different cultures to understand the Bible better and to know the fullness of Christ. After all, in order for us to know God more fully, God sent Jesus as a human being born in a historical and cultural context in Palestine. The incarnation is the theological principle that supports contextualization. The Word becomes flesh, one of us (John 1:14). The Word must become flesh in every local cultural context. Likewise, the universal message of the Bible, addressed to all human beings, is translated and finds expression in every local and contextual form. The universality and fullness of the biblical message is better grasped through the rich variety of its cultural forms and translations. Here we see the local and the global come together.

There is no pure theology. All theology is developed in some particular cultural context. The cradle of Christianity was in the Near East, but Jewish Christians like Paul soon began to use the language of the Greco-Roman world in order to reach that world with the message. John's use of the "Word" (Logos) is one example. After the first millennium, Christianity formally split into Eastern and Western traditions. Western theology developed in the universities. The modern missionary movement was at a peak as the second millennium approached its end. It was inevitably influenced by the colonialism and paternalism of the North American and European Protestant and Catholic cultures. As we entered the third millennium, the flourishing of contextual theologies and missiologies resulted in such growth of the church in the Southern hemisphere that "majority" or representative world Christianity now is non-Western. Local congregations everywhere are constructing local theologies and missiologies. The mystery of God's mission takes on exciting dimensions!

Contextualization is not relativism. In the introduction of *Constants in Context*, Stephen Bevans and Roger Schroeder state that theology and church history are "shaped by the constant but always contextual Christian biblical and doctrinal traditions." Furthermore, the task of all Christian mission is to "preserve, defend, and proclaim the *constants* of the church's traditions; at the same time it must respond creatively and boldly to the *contexts* in which it finds itself." Christian history is "a story of the encounter of Eternal Word with changing worlds" or "a story of *constants* in *context*." The challenge today is "to construct a theology that is inspired by God's constant missionary action in the world."[9] Vincent Donovan, Catholic missioner among the Masai in East Africa, explains contextualization as "planting the seed of faith and allowing it to interact with the native soil, leading to a new flowering of Christianity, faithful both to the local culture and to the apostolic faith."[10]

A key question is posed: Who constructs local theologies? My students at the seminary of the Independent Presbyterian Church of Brazil in Londrina taught me valuable lessons about contextualization. Local communities and national churches take responsibility for examining their own context or reality and for shaping a culturally relevant and appropriate response to the gospel. Their insistence on reading the culture alongside the text has helped me to develop my own missiology and to correct many of my mistakes. I was always fascinated by how much space my students dedicated to the significance of Galilee in their New Testament theses. In my theological training I had never thought much about the significance of Jesus concentrating his ministry in the poorest, peripheral, multicultural and multireligious region, far from the center of power in Jerusalem. Living and ministering in a cross-cultural context is challenging. It is a journey to an increasingly fuller vision of God's cosmic mission.

I find that many local congregations from the United States, in their partnerships with presbyteries and local congregations in other contexts, have not been trained to understand the importance of contextualization. Some simply take their own agendas and American ways of doing things to other countries. These agendas may have nothing to do with the agenda of the congregations they visit. Their systematic work style and reluctance to "waste time" in just being with people can result in misunderstandings. Some congregations with good hearts and intentions think that models of evangelism from the North should work in struggling congregations in the South or in Islamic countries. I attended a workshop on Brazil at a conference once in the United States where two women from the United States explained the Brazilian mission context while at least four eager Brazilian mission leaders remained silent spectators. That was a serious mistake!

I suggest that local congregations engaging in cross-cultural mission equip themselves first and foremost with the attitudes of humility and respect. We go as guests, followers, and learners. We listen, observe, and learn as much as we can about the local culture, customs, history, religions, church, theology, liturgy, mission, social relationships, folklore, and ways of living and communicating. We should demonstrate the maximum respect for all we see even when we do not understand or agree. We should participate in as many local cultural practices as possible. We should interact with local people on their terms. We should get to know one another.

When local congregations cross borders and engage in mission in places where we are guests and strangers, we should always seek the help of local partners. Whenever possible, we should seek to work on projects together at their invitation, to fit into their agendas, to respect and learn from their way of doing theology, liturgy, and mission. Contextual theology and mission are a shift in perspective for people who have never been outside their own context. Usually we have to rid ourselves of negative cultural baggage when we practice cross-cultural mission. In turn, we are transformed and enriched as we give and receive positive cultural gifts.

The Global Church in Local-Global Mission

Some local congregations in the North that engage in global mission in other countries fail to recognize the presence and significance of the global church today. They are not prepared to accept the new role of the global church in local-global mission. We forget that Christianity has been present in the Middle East and in countries like Ethiopia, Albania, and India since the beginning of the Christian era and in China since the seventh century. We fail to celebrate and reflect on the fact that today Christianity is a world religion, present in every country in the world. Furthermore, as Philip Jenkins demonstrates in *The Next Christendom: The Coming of Global Christianity*, during the course of the twentieth century "the center of gravity in the Christian world has shifted inexorably southward, to Africa, Asia, and Latin America. Already today, the largest Christian communities on the planet are to be found in Africa and Latin America."[11]

Mission today is ecumenical because the church that started in Jerusalem is now a global church with strong autonomous denominations and local congregations doing mission in six continents. The global church is made up of Catholic, Orthodox, Protestant, and Pentecostal churches. The majority of Christians in the Global South are poor and members of one of the myriad varieties of Pentecostal churches. Why is there such explosive church growth in the Global South while many churches in the North continue to decline? One of the reasons is that most Christians in the Global South, especially Pentecostals, are actively committed and involved in practices of evangelism alongside social ministries. According to Ian T. Douglas, this is not simply a "result of the globalization of Western churches but rather the ongoing movement of the Spirit of God released at Pentecost."[12]

Slowly, Christians in the North are waking up to the reality that the majority church today is composed of Southern Christians in Latin America, Africa, and Asia. The majority Southern church now is shaping mission theology and practice and providing leadership for the global mission movement. Churches in South Korea, India, Nigeria, and Brazil are sending great numbers of cross-cultural mission workers to other countries. Indeed, churches in the Global South are shaping the ecumenical mission agenda. The global church is a primary actor of God's mission today.

We are learning to recognize the fact that the majority of the followers of Jesus Christ around the world are not of our theological and cultural tradition. In his next book, *The New Faces of Christianity: Believing the Bible in the Global South*, Philip Jenkins reminds us that not only has the demographic center of the church shifted to the South, but the conservative and even fundamentalist reading and understanding of the Bible also is now the prevalent view.[13] We simply cannot impose our scriptural interpretations on others. This is a real challenge. We must humbly admit that there are many ways of understanding, celebrating, and living God's revelation in Jesus Christ. Furthermore, we must accept the fact that each church in each local community and nation has the primary responsibility for local mission in their community, nation, and region. In countries where there are faithful autonomous national churches and councils of churches, we need to be open to support their initiatives, receive their contributions and invitations, and cooperate with them in mission in their regions and in other places.

When people comprehend the reality of the global church in local mission, they often ask fundamental questions: Is there still a need for cross-cultural global mission? Is there a reason for local congregations anywhere to engage in global mission? If the global church is engaged in mission, why do we need to leave our local communities and support mission in other places? If we respect the religions and cultures of others, why should we do mission in their locations? Why not simply allow every local congregation everywhere in the global church to do local mission in their own local community and region? If the global church in the Southern hemisphere now is the leader in global mission, is there still a role and need for the church in the North to do global mission?

Connecting Mission Near and Far in One Universal Body

In our globalized world, it is not hard to perceive that all Christians are members of *both* a local faith community *and* the global church. We all belong to the one universal body of Christ. We join sisters and brothers who recite the Nicene Creed in hundreds of languages and places and affirm that all local congregations together form the "one holy catholic apostolic church." The church is catholic because there is one global church, and it is particular

because there are many local congregations in many places. All of our partner relationships in global mission remind us that each local congregation
shares in and needs the full catholicity of the universal body of Christ.

Twelve years after publishing *Constructing Local Theologies*, Robert J.
Schreiter wrote *The New Catholicity*.[14] In it he seeks to discover what has
happened to the meaning of "context" in a globalized world, where homog-
enizing forces of global capitalism and communication impact local situations. For example, McDonald's fast food, information technology, and the
Internet have changed our world. Fast food, music, movies, fashion, sports,
video games, and the World Wide Web have united people around the globe
in a new global culture. At the same time, paradoxically, ethnic and religious
forces continue to divide groups like Israelis and Palestinians, and Sunni and
Shiite Muslims. Additionally, "new particularisms," such as the divisions of
the former Yugoslavia or consumer choices (how to get your coffee, etc.),
have become strong definers of identity.

The new theological framework that Schreiter offers for living between
the global and the local comes from the concept of catholicity. He shows
us how catholicity means that each local community is a part of the global
church and only finds wholeness and fullness of faith and mission through
intense dialogue and intercultural exchange. This requires two-way mission
and missionary dialogue in holistic mission both locally and globally. All
local congregations need mutual local, regional, national, ecumenical, and
global partners in God's one mission. A congregation that practices only
local mission without commitment to the global church (or vice versa) will
never experience the fullness of God's mission. Consequently, its identity
is incomplete.

I have been greatly enriched by the writings of Leonardo Boff. He teaches
us that the catholicity of the church points to our responsibility to respect
and receive the spiritual gifts and particularities of other congregations.[15] In
Planetary Civilization,[16] Boff says that the complex process of globalization,
the revolution of information and communication in which we are one and
diverse, has given us a new collective consciousness. We are part of a new
global society, with diverse churches, religions, and cultures, that demands
interdependence, coresponsibility, reconnections, holism, and integration.
Boff suggests that Christianity of liberation, solidarity, and dialogue can promote this new collective planetary consciousness. We must be liberated from
cultures of domination and all that hinders God's plan for living together in
mutuality and solidarity. We must break down all barriers of isolation, misun-
derstanding, prejudice, and discrimination incongruent with the holy catholic
church. Together we then can experience the fullness of life that God intends

for persons and for the universe in God's cosmic mission plan. Boff reminds us that the resurrection of Christ is the first sign of this life in fullness.

We begin to participate in God's mission in a partial way in one local community. Then God also sends us to go beyond, to cross borders, and eventually to become global Christians in a global church. All baptized Christians and all local congregations engage in cross-cultural mission situations as we seek to understand and dialogue with the culture(s) in our communities and around the world. When we leave our comfort zones and engage in intercultural communication and communion, whether locally or globally, we are mutually challenged and changed. As people of different places, cultures, classes, languages, and ages minister to one another in one universal Christian fellowship, sharing their cultural expressions and gifts, we enter into fullness of life and mission. Furthermore, Ian T. Douglas affirms that "connecting, one to one, individual to individual, local church to local church, across the divides of culture, race, ethnicity, and geography, is a radical act of participation in God's ongoing incarnation."[17] Even when we have significant theological, methodological, or cultural differences, the faith-sharing approach of pilgrims on the way nurtures seeds of faith, bringing growth to all.

Synergy and Convergence in Local-Global Mission

Jack Haberer wrote an editorial in *The Presbyterian Outlook* in 2007 on "Mission Convergence," urging the many diverse sectors of the Presbyterian Church (U.S.A.) to unite around the identity of a "missional church." I applaud and join Jack in this appeal as I advocate partnership and unity in mission. As a contribution, I would like to revisit and update what I wrote about the "Local-Global Symbiosis" in 2000.[18] Furthermore, I suggest that we need mission structures that enable all mission participants of the PC(USA) engaged in local or global mission in the areas of evangelism, compassion, or social justice to do so from the perspective of the greater picture of God's holistic local-global mission. In this convergence model we recognize and value all ministries in all places and the rich fullness of initiators and participants in God's mission. We realize that all issues are global in our totally interconnected biosphere and that we have become a multi-everything global community.

The issue is stated by Robert Schreiter: "Can the Church of Jesus Christ balance the global and the local, with all the implications implied therein?"[19] What does it mean for all of us to work as partners in mutual mission in order to achieve synergy and convergence between local and global mission?

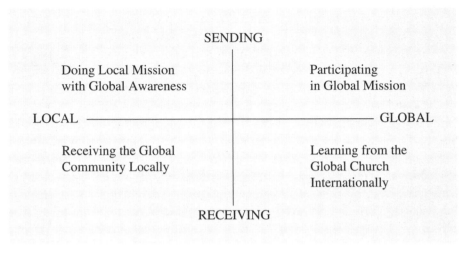

Fig. 3.2. The Local-Global Symbiosis

I offer four concrete guidelines of the interaction of two axes of mission: global-local and sending-receiving (see fig. 3.2).[20] Use these guidelines to evaluate and design your total mission plan.

1. *Congregations do local mission outside the front door with an awareness of the presence of the global community near and far, with a special concern for least reached and marginalized peoples, and with a perception of the global implications of all issues.*

When I say "outside the front door," I do not mean that you cease using your facilities for missional activities, such as soup kitchens, twelve-step programs, interfaith hospitality for the homeless, second-language classes, and day care. To the contrary, I hope you do this more and more, seven days a week. However, we cannot forget that God calls the church to gather for worship and sacraments and then sends us out into the world in mission. Our primary mission field today is not distant lands but our own backyard, our own neighborhood, our own city, our own county. It is hypocritical to participate in worldwide mission and not share the gospel with the invisible groups of people in our own communities. How is this global? The world is at our doorstep. The church has often unconsciously erected barriers that prohibit us from recognizing, inviting, welcoming, and building relationships with people from all nations in our communities. Our international neighbors can help us minister to new immigrants and be global Christians who grasp the global implications of the things we consume and of the political actions we support. A Presbyterian mission statement reminds us: "Helping people link their reality to that of people throughout the world can deepen faith, shape vocational choices, and change society."[21]

This is why your mission department needs to provide this global perspective for all committees, task forces, or teams organized for specific local mission programs. The ministry goals of these task forces must challenge them to think globally as they act locally. When local task forces meet, they need to see and reflect on where the world is present in their area of ministry. Each member might share the stories of any international neighbors or companions in the workplace. These people can become valuable resources to the local mission team. You might invite them to share their faith journeys and the challenges they have faced as immigrants or refugees.

2. *Congregations participate in God's universal mission around the world in partnership with the global church, with an awareness of least reached and marginalized peoples, and with maximum respect, solidarity, mutuality, and hands-on involvement.*

Though the emphasis on missional activity is local, there are still the needs and opportunities for individuals and groups to join in mission with Christ's global church. However, this is done in reciprocal relationships with partner churches. They invite us and direct the work. The Presbyterian Church (U.S.A.) continues to receive invitations from over 160 partner denominations around the world. Requests also come from ecumenical agencies and theological institutions, councils of churches, nongovernmental organizations, and others to participate in local/national/regional/global mission together. Additionally, there are challenges and opportunities for frontier mission in places where there is no indigenous Christian community.

However, it is urgent for Western missionaries to learn that they must no longer impose their own agendas and culture when they go to other countries. Local congregations and presbyteries in the North persevere with their partners in the South as they struggle to learn together and develop mutual mission relationships with authenticity and integrity. We must go with humility, as invited guests who show respect for our hosts. This engagement ranges from two-week mission trips by groups, to short-term work by mission volunteers, to long-term assignments in response to invitations of partners. Though Robert Schreiter suggests that we are moving beyond the "period of solidarity" (1945–1989) to the "period of globalization" (1989–),[22] I think mutuality and solidarity still characterize the paradigm we must follow. This is why, in *Called as Partners in Christ's Service*, I insist on dyads of mutual practices: listening and speaking, learning and teaching, receiving and giving. Of all of these, receiving is especially hard for us from the United States to learn.

Many local congregations have a strong commitment and mobilization in both national and international mission. I often consult by e-mail with church mission committees that wish to form new international partnerships or do short-term trips. I also see the requests of national partner churches and church leaders throughout South America for financial or other types of support for projects, programs, institutions, or personnel. I challenge people to make wise choices, to learn from history, to see the big picture, and to put into practice effective missiological principles.

3. *Congregations receive the global community locally, from near and far, as God's gifts and missionary agents to them.*

Jesus received the service and gifts of Peter's mother-in-law, Martha, Mary Magdalene, and many other people. We should view persons from other countries, who are in our country for a myriad of reasons and whose stay is temporary or generational, not only as persons to be reached and embraced evangelistically but also as ones who bring spiritual gifts and might reevangelize us and teach us. In an age of massive population movements (emigration, immigration, refugees) it is obvious that global is not only geographical. Crucial attitudes in an ecclesiology of multiculturalism are mutual transformation, openness, receptivity, and hospitality. We must broaden our partnerships with ethnic congregations, open our facilities to immigrant fellowships, and venture forth creatively to become multicultural churches. From Korean Americans we can learn much about prayer; from African Americans we can discover new vitality for worship and social justice; and from Latin Americans we can deepen our understanding of hospitality and evangelism. The globalization of theological education has resulted in international exchanges of students and professors. The Mission to the U.S.A. Program of the Presbyterian Church (U.S.A.) receives mission workers from many countries as missionaries in the United States. There are countless possibilities that might hold the keys to renewal and revitalization of your church!

For many years, Victor Makari has served the PC(USA) denominational mission agencies with a global perspective. This native of Egypt leads worship, bringing enriching gifts from one of the cradles of Christianity. Victor is astutely aware of the complexities of relationships throughout South Asia and the Middle East. He understands the needs and requests of our partners. Victor's ministry as area coordinator for the Middle East is a real gift to the PC(USA).

4. *Congregations experience the global church internationally and allow Christian messages, values, and practices learned from brothers and sisters in other contexts to continually nurture and transform them.*

One of the basic assumptions of this book is that there is one global church, and every Christian is a member of it. With the facilities of intercontinental travel and communication media, many members of local congregations have the resources to experience the global church in other countries. Great care must be taken as individuals and groups travel or spend time abroad so that they do not perpetuate the famous culturally insensitive "Ugly American" image of the 1950s. Cross-cultural mission is a difficult task. Yet God's Spirit can prepare us. Moreover, by emptying ourselves of all attitudes of superiority, greatness, and condescendence, we can patiently listen to English with foreign accents and tentatively experiment with phrases in other languages. As we go, we open ourselves to hear different interpretations of Scripture and corrective prophetic messages that reveal our blind spots. We discover values in other cultures, ideologies, and religions that resonate with the claims of the gospel message and that often challenge certain cultural values we hold dear that do not resonate with the claims of the gospel. As we worship, pray, play, work, and have table fellowship with sisters and brothers around the globe, we will be challenged, encouraged, inspired, and transformed.

In my years as a mission worker, professor, mission consultant, and regional liaison, I have observed many mistakes and misguided attitudes in people with good intentions. I have also witnessed an abundance of skills, resources, willingness, and talents of people from many local congregations who visit and form partnerships in other countries. I have seen seeds sown in good soil that have "produced a hundredfold" (Luke 8:8), bringing joy and growth to many. Ministry that is of lasting value is demanding. In visits to congregations, through correspondence, at mission conferences, and in publications, I have provided missiological orientation to individuals, congregations, committees, volunteers in mission, and colleagues. Don't engage in global mission service without first preparing yourself. It is a lifelong learning process and adventure. Equip the mission leaders and participants in your congregation. More than good hearts and intentions must guide us. The preparation is worth it!

Chapter 4

What Does the Bible Say about Mission?

One Holistic Mission: Biblical and Theological Reflection on Ephesians

I am a pastor in a congregation founded more than 300 years ago by French Huguenots and Reformed Christians from various parts of Germany. Being the only Reformed church in the region, it forms a small synod together with a few others of comparable history and tradition, which we would call congregational. Through all the centuries my congregation has been as independent as its sister congregations have been. These congregations are strong in the sense that they always carried a great responsibility for their work and mission, for which a certain commitment of the congregants was needed and has always been given. So far, so good.

But then there is the Evangelical Reformed Church, a much bigger church in Germany we are cooperating with. We are not yet a part or member congregation of it. There is no theological reason for still being divided; we share the same confessions and basic principles. In contrast, there are many reasons to become one, to unite. But until now all attempts to merge failed because of different structures, which did not seem to be compatible, and because of a certain kind of fear on both sides to compromise on what we are used to and what we want to preserve. If it were for personal interest, it wouldn't matter. What matters is that we weaken our witness we are called to give as a church to the world—and this seemingly because we are afraid of belonging and having to bear distinctiveness and diversity.

Unity means the contrary of self-assertion: being part of, being next to someone, experiencing togetherness, being responsible, accountable, and yet cared for.

Unity is not made by us but is a gift. In God's Spirit we become one. And we are urged to treasure and to keep this unity, to live according to this togetherness, to live in reliance on our sisters and brothers. In so doing, we respond to the call received from Christ.[1]

How can the Bible guide us in mission today? Is the Bible a missionary document? What does the Bible say about our calling as Christians and as the church? Why is it better to do mission together? Is Christian unity a part of God's mission design as revealed in the Scriptures?

Discovering a Holistic Methodology

Every book has an organizing methodology. In this book my organizing plan comes from a treasure I have discovered in over thirty years of learning from theologians and Bible interpreters in Latin America. In my experience as a Presbyterian Church (U.S.A.) mission coworker and missiologist, I have learned to think biblically about God's missionary action in context and to analyze theologically the origin, source, motives, and practices of God's mission.

Latin Americans use a circular method of reading the Bible. What is more holistic or whole than a circle? Where does a circle begin? Where does it end? It keeps going round and round. There are two basic elements in the Latin American interpretative approach: the context and the text. It takes seriously God's Word and God's world. The Bible is the text, and we come to this text with our own text: our personal experience and our cultural context. These things are necessary to make the biblical text come alive. However, if we only interpret the Bible according to our own text, we will miss out on much that is there. Yet if every culture examines the Bible with its own perspective and we all share in the result, we are all much more likely to come closer to the truth.

The new wineskin for Latin American missiology is that we begin with the context, with our present reality. We begin with our mission practice, which includes our mistakes and our many unanswered questions. We admit our frustrations and limitations. We examine our missional reality. This requires an analysis of the community and of the greater context. We name our practices. We do a reality check.

My methodological goal in the first three chapters was to engage and compel readers—local congregations, denominational leaders, mission practitioners everywhere—to pull you into the circle of missiological reflection and dialogue. I started each chapter with case studies and questions. I sought to enable you to identify and examine the feet-on-the ground challenges, questions, and important missiological issues we face in today's world. I tried to lead you in an honest critical analysis of your church's mission practices. I am passionate about God's mission and about the church's participation in it.

However, sometimes I feel like a gadfly. I find encouragement in David Bosch's words: "missiology acts as a gadfly in the house of theology, creating unrest and resisting complacency, opposing every ecclesiastical impulse to self-preservation, every desire to stay what we are, every inclination toward provincialism and parochialism, every fragmentation of humanity. . . . Missiology's task, furthermore, is critically to accompany the missionary enterprise, to scrutinize its foundations, its aims, attitude, message, and methods."[2]

This chapter moves around the circle to focus now on the biblical text. It intends to help church members listen to the Word of God and to reflectively discern missiological themes. We bring our reality, our critical analysis, our questions, and our suspicions to the Word of God. We listen to the message of the Bible to see what God says to us today in our context, what God requires of us, what changes God wants to make in us, where God is leading us in mission. We hear the biblical message not only as individuals, but also as members of our own ecclesial tradition and of the church universal. We only comprehend the fullness of God's biblical revelation with a fullness of cultural perspectives and interpretations, if then.

For this reason we listen to the collective wisdom of the global church and of our church tradition as it interprets Scripture and analyzes contexts. Our biblical interpretation is richer because it is missiological and ecumenical. My tradition is the Presbyterian Church (U.S.A.), a branch of the Reformed tradition, a part of the church universal. Other traditions can learn from mine even as I have learned from listening to others. In this dialogical process we never lose our particular identity, but we learn better together. By bringing our contextual analysis to a missionary dialogue with the biblical text, we keep moving around the circle with resulting new practices, new wine in new wineskins, as we go forth in holistic local-global mission.

To give a holistic view of what Scripture says to us about mission, I would cover the whole Bible, beginning with Genesis 1 and God's good creation, observing the table of nations in Genesis 11, and stressing God's commission to Abraham in Genesis 12 to be a blessing to all the nations. There is much more in the Hebrew Scriptures, and the Gospels portray the mission of Jesus, which is passed on to the disciples. Acts shows the church discovering its universal missional vocation. In Revelation are glimpses of the goal of God's cosmic mission plan. But space will not permit a study of the missionary vision in the whole Bible (see summary in fig. 4.1).[3] So I ask: Which book in the Bible presents the most developed vision of the church-in-mission? I

GOD'S GOOD WORLD	ELECTION OF ISRAEL	INCARNATION	PENTECOST	UNIVERSAL KINGDOM
CREATION (Gen. 1–2)	for Mission to Nations	God **Sends** Savior "Flesh-on" Mission (John 1:14; 3:16)	God **Sends** Spirit To Empower the Church for Mission to All Nations (Acts 2)	REIGN OF GOD CONSUMMATION COSMIC RENEWAL
FALL (Gen. 3)	Promises to Abraham, Moses, and David	Jesus inaugurates the reign of God (Luke 4:17–19)		"Then people will come from east and west, from north and south, and will eat in the kingdom of God." (Luke 13:29)
MISSIONAL CONCERN "Where are you?" (Gen. 3:9)	"In you all the families of the earth shall be blessed." (Gen. 12:3)	Evangelizes, meets human needs, and challenges social injustices	"Through the church the wisdom of God in its rich variety might now be made known to the rulers and authorities in the heavenly places." (Eph. 3:10)	"[God has] a plan for the fullness of time, to gather up all things in [Christ], things in heaven, and things on earth." (Eph. 1:10)
PROMISES TO THE WHOLE WORLD (Gen. 3:15, 21; 9:15–16)	Israel misunderstood its missional identity and turned inward	Forms a Community and **sends** them to "make disciples" (Matt. 28:19–20; John 20:21; Acts 1:8)	"Be filled with the Spirit." (Eph. 5:18)	"the river of the water of life. . . . the healing of the nations" (Rev. 22:1–2)
ONE CREATOR ONE HUMAN RACE MANY NATIONS AND CULTURES (Gen. 11)	Psalms and Prophets remember and envision the nations in God's reign	God "has put all things under his feet and has made him the head over all things for the church, which is his body, the fullness of him who fills all in all." (Eph. 1:22–23)	The church is one body, called and sent into the world on a mission to represent the reign of God as Sign, Foretaste, Agent, and Instrument	Integrity of all Creation Shalom Justice Peace Love
GOD'S UNIVERSAL MISSION of Restoration Salvation Liberation	"I am coming to gather all nations and tongues; and they shall come and shall see my glory, and I will set a sign among them." (Isa. 66:18–19) LIGHT TO THE NATIONS (Isa. 42:6)	DEATH RESURRECTION FULLNESS OF LIFE ASCENSION	Has the church understood its identity?	Worship and Celebration

Fig. 4.1. God's Mission in the Bible

think it is the Letter to the Ephesians. Let's look at the whole book to catch a holistic vision of the missional themes in it.

What does Ephesians teach us about God's mission? This letter overwhelms us with the fullness of God's redemptive and reconciling mission. It paints with broad strokes on a huge canvas; and it paints the big picture, the length and breadth of God's holistic, cosmic mission. A missiological reading of Ephesians is breathtaking, challenging, and encouraging. The themes—breaking down walls, reconciliation, unity in mission, relationships of love, and cooperation in the body—have eternal relevance and are particularly apt today.

Some say that Paul wrote the Letter to the Ephesians from his prison cell; others maintain that it was written much later by one or some of his disciples who carried on his story, claimed his authority, and further developed his ecclesiology. To me, that would be a supreme sign of the fruits of Paul's mission work. Likewise, some insist that it was written to the Christian community at Ephesus; others maintain with equal conviction that it was a circular letter intended for many churches planted by Paul in Asia Minor. It is not my purpose to engage these issues here because these disputes do not matter for the purposes of my argument. Still, as a mission worker who knows the importance of writing periodic newsletters to churches, I like the circular letter idea. A letter about the fullness of God's mission in the world needs as broad an audience as possible. The vital thing for us to keep in mind is that this letter was written either to a local Christian community engaged in mission or to a group of local congregations that were also interested in mission in nearby regions.

Act 1: Ephesians 1:3–2:10

The Fullness of God's Cosmic Mission

In a lecture to seminarians titled "The Top Ten Reasons to Put the Great Commission at the Heart of Your Ministry," Marian McClure's first point was to "focus on the big picture of God's mission."[4] In Ephesians 1–3 we see a broad perspective, the entire range of God's eternal plan, Christ's redemptive mission worked out in and beyond history. It begins "before the foundation of the world" (1:4), moves forward in love, gains momentum, and then on the big screen suddenly appears "the mystery of [God's] will . . . in Christ, as a plan for the fullness of time, to gather up all things in [Christ], things in heaven and things on earth" (1:9–10). In today's language, "to gather up" would be to use a calculator or computer program "to sum up" numbers at the end of a column in order to present one coherent whole.[5] We see our loving Maker clicking on a divine computer program that gathers up, sums up, unites, and brings together all human creatures and all of creation under a single head, the Lord of all life, Jesus Christ. Our Sovereign God is in control of the whole created order. God has a plan. The ultimate goal of history and of God's mission is cosmic renewal and the unity of God's people and universe. God desires the complete humanity of all people. We will be whole!

This is the biblical vision behind the Presbyterian Church's statement *Gathering for God's Future*. God's mission is cosmic, universal, and holistic. Mission is summing up and integrating many parts into the whole design. Holistic mission gathers together evangelism, witness, compassionate service, social justice, and the integrity of creation. There is an important missiological lesson here. We must be careful not to create dichotomies or neglect any part of God's gathering. The "mystery" of God's will includes unification and integration. Now prepare yourself for the breathtaking surprise that explodes in verses 22 and 23 of Ephesians 1.

"And [God] has put *all* things under [Christ's] feet and has made him the head over *all* things [are you ready?] for the church, which is [Christ's] body, [there's more!] the fullness of him who fills *all* in *all*" (stress added). After acknowledging the universal lordship of Jesus Christ over the cosmos, we discover that God's mission has a church, the body of Christ incarnated in all of history. Mission is the church´s participation in the fullness of God, in Christ, empowered by the Spirit. The church is part and participant of God's mission, "created for good works" (2:10), by which God's universal purpose is being realized. Furthermore, the church is the first to receive or share the fullness of Christ. Wow! How could the church be the fullness of Christ? This is only possible in fellowship with the triune God. Jesus fills the body. Now it takes all kinds of members to fill or complete the body of Christ. Without the diversity of different parts, it will never be full. Through the church the fullness of God is then shared with the rest of creation. This is the scope and mystery of God's purpose for the church.

What an awesome and majestic vision and great responsibility! John Stott says that Christ fills the church and the universe. The church is his "body," and he directs it; the church is his "fullness," and he fills it.[6] "So fill 'er up!" Yes, we're empty. We leak. We can do nothing on our own. We are intrinsically selfish, with self-interests and mixed motives. The prayer and exhortation in Ephesians are appropriate: "that you may be filled with all the fullness of God" (3:19) and "be filled with the Spirit" (5:18).

A thread that runs throughout Ephesians is the Greek word *plērōma*, which means "rich fullness," "totality," "to fill something completely," "to fulfill." God fills, fulfills, completes, and reaches out to all things. Later in this chapter we will see that Christ in fullness dispenses the gifts of grace. God's fullness includes God's mission and the gift of partnership with humanity and creation. God is filling all things. This results in fullness of spiritual and physical life and dignity for all. Many Latin Americans understand mission in these terms. God's mission means fullness of glacier springs for Bolivia, fullness of human rights in Colombia, fullness of reconciliation in Peru, fullness of food security in Africa, fullness of environmental safety in China. Nelson Mandela, Martin Luther King Jr., and Mother Teresa represent the dream of fullness of life and dignity for all. This is why the fullness of God's mission includes evangelism, compassion, and justice and has a full range of active participants or "mission initiators" everywhere.

In the big picture, we see God gathering up and filling all things and also lavishing grace. Yes, grace is "freely bestowed" (1:6) and "lavished" (1:8). In Christ we are recipients of the "immeasurable riches of [God's] grace" (2:7). Grace is "the gift of God" (2:8; 3:7–8). In Ephesians 2:1–10, we discover that God's mission is altogether gift. The triune God is "inexhaustible Giver, Given, and Gift/ing through love."[7] We receive God's gift of grace and respond to it in loving relationships with God and others. The source of mission is God's grace, God's gifts, God's love, God's fullness. Michael Downey poetically describes "God's superabundant life pouring itself forth, the love of God who gives and gives again but is never emptied in the giving: . . . the utter gratuity of life and love, in God's constant coming as gift." God is relational, personal, "not a self-contained individual . . . God is not turned in; nor is God . . . self-imposed, self-selecting, blissful isolation. . . . God's very life is the relationality and mutual self-gift that makes Love what it is."[8] What other mission motivation can compare?

We are simply electrified by this mission text, which is God's response to humankind's dilemma: "But God, who is rich in mercy, out of the great love with which God loved us, . . . made us alive together with Christ" (2:4). The implications of God's grace and power at work in the resurrection are clear. Life defeats death! Fullness of life with dignity is for all! The source of mission is the divine gracious initiative, the flowing of mercy, the pouring forth of the love and life of God. To say that "God is love" is to affirm the partnership principles of mutuality and interdependence. Divine love invites us to practice the discipline of receptivity. Rightly understood, this leads to a missiology of no competitiveness and to a mission practice of togetherness. Carola Tron, Waldensian pastor in Uruguay, bears witness to the far-reaching consequences: "The grace of God transforms us into new persons; grace involves repentance and forgiveness. . . . Grace is a new way of living and understanding life under God's blessing. . . . Grace is a new model of God's economy. . . . We are called to live in the grace of God that is connected with all creation."[9] Mission is shared grace.

Act 2: Ephesians 2:11–22

The Unity of God's Reconciled Church

The missional plan of the God of grace, who is gathering up and filling the body of Christ and the universe, envisions the creation of one body. The unity of the triune God is a model and source of the unity of the church. How is this seemingly impossible unity achieved? In Ephesians we discover that the risen Christ "has broken down the dividing wall" (2:14). Yes, this is God's mission at work—breaking down walls of hostility between people and creating in Christ "one new humanity in place of the two, thus making peace," reconciling "both groups to God in one body through the cross" (2:15–16). It is only God in Christ who offers and makes peace and reconciliation possible. We receive these gifts and become participants in reconciled and reconciling communities (2 Cor. 5:17–19). God's mission practices include breaking down walls, creating one body, one Christian family, reconciling us to God and to one another, and making peace. If these are not our practices, we are not participating in God's mission. God has entrusted the church with a mission of reconciliation. There must be no barriers that separate us in Christ.

The historical division and metaphorical wall described in Ephesians was between Jewish and Gentile Christians. The first Christian community was composed of Jews who followed Jesus as Messiah and maintained many Jewish customs. God's universal mission then brought Gentile believers into the fold. It was difficult for the Hebrew Christians with conscious sectarian attitudes of superiority to accept Gentiles, especially as equals. They were two different extremes going in opposite directions. There seemed to be no meeting point. However, according to the renowned Scottish missiologist Andrew Walls, for "a few brief years . . . the irreconcilables were reconciled," and this is a model to be repeated.[10] Unity through Christ and in Christ connects extremes. This is a marvelous and wondrous miracle! Walls uses the image of the dividing wall between Hebrews and Gentiles, the building metaphors at the end of Ephesians 2, and the body metaphor to show how central this message is in the entire book:

> The Epistle to the Ephesians shows how the two have been made one through Christ's cross. Here are not simply two races, but two lifestyles, two cultures, and, different as they are, they belong to each other. Each is a building block

in a new temple that is in process of building; nay, each is an organ in a functioning body of which Christ is the brain. The Temple will not be completed, the Body will not function, unless both are present. Moreover, Christ is full humanity, and it is only together that we reach his full stature.[11]

By 325 CE the church was cross-cultural in its makeup, and Gentiles had become the majority in the church. A significant paradigm shift from a Hebrew cultural mind-set to a Greco-Roman world vision had taken place. It was a dramatic change. The church today has experienced another complex change. There has been a demographic shift in which the majority of Christians now live in the Global South. This is resulting in the cultural transformation of Christianity from a Western to a non-Western religion. Missiologists today affirm that these changes are as great as the the shift from the Hebrew mother church to Gentile Christianity in the second century, and as great as the Protestant Reformation in the sixteenth century. Furthermore, the Southern majority church now is assuming an increasing responsibility for the evangelization of the world.

What are the implications of God's practice of breaking down walls for mission today? Cuban theologians Ofelia Ortega and Marcos Cruz offer important insights: "Our witness needs unity, as it is the way in which it can be truly fruitful. Behind this truth, however, lies an even deeper truth. If we are not capable of giving a witness of peace among us—one in which the walls separating us crumble down and the prejudices keeping us aloof are overcome—then we are not fully living our own reconciliation with God."[12] Many Christians in Cuba and the United States are united in their prayers to bring down the diplomatic and economic walls that divide their countries.

Consider some of the walls built in the world. Both the building and the tearing down of the Berlin Wall had tremendous consequences in the world and in mission. Today there are many frontier mission workers in countries that were previously isolated by the "Iron Curtain." For example, American Presbyterians are establishing relations with the emerging house churches in all the formerly USSR "stan" countries (Kazakhstan, Kyrgyzstan, Tajikistan, Turkmenistan, and Uzbekistan). The wall that is being built between Mexico and the United States is a sad symbol of our nation's failure to deal peacefully and diplomatically with immigration issues. The wall built by Israel makes the daily lives of many Palestinians a nightmare and peaceful two-state solutions extremely hard.

Unfortunately, our difficulty in understanding the roots of the animosity of Arab nations and extremist groups against the United States and our fear of more terrorist attacks are making our borders into walls and turning our embassies from entryways into fortresses. This in turn contributes to the "clash of civilizations" described in Samuel P. Huntington's book, *The Clash of Civilizations and the Remaking of World Order*, or the rising wall between East and West, and between Islam and Christianity.[13] The economic bubble and crisis that burst in 2008 places capitalism over against the leftist antiglobalization movements around the world.

And what walls are we building rather than breaking down in the church? John Stott asks, "How dare we build walls of partition in the one and only human community in which Christ has destroyed them?"[14] The division, separation, and strife in the church, universally and locally, are disturbing and shocking. Barriers of our making must be broken down from our side. We must be willing to be healed of the disease of divisiveness. We need to discover how to cooperate in God's mission of reconciliation. The ecumenical movement embraces this calling and seeks to assist churches.

The teaching of the Letter to the Ephesians on the Jewish-Gentile relationship in the body instructs us in North-South or West–non-Western partnerships in world Christianity today. Ephesians becomes paradigmatic: "The Gentiles have become fellow heirs, members of the same body, and sharers in the promise in Christ Jesus through the gospel" (3:6). We do mission not *for* others, but *with* others, seeing and listening to others as subjects and agents of mission. "Jews remain Jews and Gentiles remain Gentiles. But *inequality* before God is abolished."[15] Fellow heirs in the Northern and Southern church are equals! In God's family, rich churches and poor churches are equals!

The 215th General Assembly of the Presbyterian Church (U.S.A.) adopted the vision statement *Gathering for God's Future* (2003), which has become the basis for mission recruitment, as well as covenant agreements with partner churches and among very diverse mission-initiating groups. *Gathering for God's Future* affirms five core commitments of the Presbyterian Church (U.S.A.) in world mission. The first one is "Joining in Partnership." Three essential practices in partnerships of equals are sharing, learning, and listening. Those with more material resources or structures of power must free themselves from attitudes of domination, superiority, and entitlement and learn the best practices of true sharing. Sharing information with one another is vital. This leads to the commitment of "Sharing People and Resources" creatively and with mutual accountability. The flow of people in all directions is like the circulatory system of the body of Christ.

Many churches and mission agencies today envision shared structures in a denomination, among denominations, and with overseas partners. The strength, maturity, courage, missionary force, and vision of mission partners around the world are inspiring. They have much to share. The most difficult challenge before church mission structures from the North who send mission coworkers into our postcolonial world is to ask the hard questions and learn from the majority church exactly what kind of mission workers they still need and want in this new era of global mission.

How do we learn to share and do mission together in ever more creative ways in our divided and globalized world? What will be the shape of mission structures for the church of tomorrow? I believe Ephesians can help us. We certainly remember that we are all members of the one family of God, that Christ Jesus is the cornerstone on which the whole building is oriented, and that "in [Christ] the whole structure is joined together and grows into a holy temple in the Lord; in whom you also are built together spiritually into a dwelling place for God" (2:21–22). Christians of all cultures are joined or fit together in harmony like musical instruments in an orchestra.

Not only are all of us in the body or temple "joined together," but we are also "built together." In other words, we grow better together! Mission, nurture, and unity are inseparable. God's holistic mission envisions "the whole structure," or church, "joined together." For this reason a third commitment in *Gathering for God's Future* is "Working Ecumenically." Andrew Walls predicts that the "great issues of twenty-first-century Christianity are likely to be ecumenical."[16] After all, Christianity has become a universal faith.

Unity in mission begins "at home," within the denomination and local Christian community. I believe that a common mission commitment can renew and unite the diverse parts of the church that, like the Jews and Gentiles, have given to each other unhealthy labels. Upon perceiving the big picture of holistic mission, we realize that those who participate in frontier evangelism or education need those who are involved in ministries of relief, development, peace, and justice. Unity in mission can enable us to rise above our divisions and rivalries. A first step is a moment of self-evaluation and self-criticism in which we might honestly ask ourselves: Are we "connectors" or "dividers"?

Once we get our act and internal partnerships together, we can move on to perhaps the most important question we face as we enter the third millennium in our multicultural and multireligious world: How do we live and work together in a world and church increasingly more pluralistic and divided?

Act 3: Ephesians 3:1–21

The Role of God's Church-in-Mission

Ephesians 3:10 again makes clear that the eternal plan of God the creator is "that through the church the wisdom of God in its rich variety might now be made known to the rulers and authorities in the heavenly places." Biblical scholar and missiologist Timothy Carriker sees the use of the phrase "heavenly places" in Ephesians (1:3, 20; 2:6; 3:10; 6:12) as an indication that Christians have one foot in each of two worlds—the spiritual realm and the social-political-historical realm. We already taste fullness of life in the spiritual realm because of the resurrection of Jesus Christ, but we also continue to struggle against "the rulers and authorities" who dominate our historical reality. There-fore, Carriker contends, a holistic and transforming missiology must be *both* spiritual/personal/individual *and* political/collective. The evangelization of the peoples of the world, including the least reached, will only be effective "within the bigger context of the redemption of the powers behind them, at the spiritual level and the socio-political level. This is one and the same task."[17] This is why our mission is *both* an announcement of good news to individuals and a social mission to denounce and transform the powers or unjust structures, systems, and ideologies that rule our world. We value persons as Jesus did, but we can-not restrict our mission endeavors to individuals. Carriker advises that we must learn to think "in collective cultural, social, political, and geographic terms." He explains that this leads us to consider ethnic groups including least reached peoples; less fortunate social groups such as abandoned children, blue-collar workers, indigenous groups, and so forth; the struggle against discrimination and every type of injustice; and geographical regions of special interest such as Eastern Europe, the Muslim world, our urban shanties, and the rural exodus.[18]

Ephesians makes it clear that God's cosmic mission has no limits. It is operative in all realms. It is certainly not limited to the church, but the church has a central place in God's plan as God's missionary to the world, an instru-ment, a partner, an agent, serving God's missional purpose. The Spirit of God chooses to work "through the church" by empowering and enabling the church for participation in God's mission.

Gathering for God's Future captures the essence of the teaching in Ephe-sians in a final summary statement about the missional community:

> The church is part of God's plan. We are called into the community of the church, and we call new disciples into that community. With Christ as our head, the church community exists for the sake of God's mission. We learn to serve in mission in a way that is faithful to the triune God. We are to model the kind of community God intends for all humanity. To be the church is to be one large mission society.[19]

This means that every denomination as a whole, along with each of its parts, is a mission society because the church at all levels exists for mission.

What is the mission of the church? According to Ephesians 3:10, God cre-ated and calls the church to make known cosmically, without limits in all spheres within and beyond all borders, the goodness, gospel, grace, and "wisdom of God in its rich variety." This last phrase could be translated "many-colored," for it is used to describe embroidered cloth, woven carpets, beautiful tapestry, or flowers. God's holistic mission of forgiveness, redemption, and healing is like a huge handmade Persian rug or the magnificent lace tablecloths sold in open-air markets in Northeast Brazil or a field of wild spring flowers in the Alps. The fullness is in the many colors and infinite designs.

The creativity and the rich diversity of God's grace and mission are greater than words can describe. God's missionary design touches the total needs of the individual, spans the entire universe, and includes many prolific dimensions of activity. It is overwhelming in its scope and variety. It invites and unites a wide gamut of mission participants, who make the compassionate Christ known and demonstrate the values of God's just and peaceful realm to persons, communities, people groups, social structures, and in the whole of creation.

In the Eastern Orthodox tradition, mission is closely associated with liturgy. Worship prepares us to engage in mission. In the Gospel narratives, Jesus' life of prayer and mission are intertwined. Prayer is mission. Prayer prepares us for mission and strengthens us to struggle against the forces of evil in our world. There is no mission without prayer. Mission is a call to pray and discern before and while acting.

In the Letter to the Ephesians, we find several prayers for the church-in-mission. In prayer the fullness of the church's role in mission pours forth:

> I pray that, according to the riches of his glory, he may grant that you may be strengthened in your inner being with power through his Spirit, and that Christ may dwell in your hearts through faith, as you are being rooted and grounded in love. I pray that you may have the power to comprehend, with all the saints, what is the breadth and length and height and depth, and to know the love of Christ that surpasses knowledge, so that you may be filled with all the fullness of God. (3:16–19)

Only in the power of the Spirit does the church exist and move out in mission. Where God's Spirit is not leading, directing, teaching, and empowering, there is no mission. Jesus is more than our missionary model; his presence within us is the enabling and driving force in mission. Our participation in God's mission only has the right motivation and attitude when we are "rooted and grounded in love." Mission is the love of God overflowing in and through us. God's mission is not merely individual or congregational or national. Why? Without the full participation of "all the saints" in their fruitful diversity and differences, we can never comprehend God's love, which is filling the church and cosmos. It requires multiple mission participants from local congregations, denominational agencies, networks, mission agencies, together with counterparts from throughout the global church, to comprehend and practice the breadth of God's mission of love. And even then we are certain to fall short.

When we contemplate the answers to the missional prayers of God's people everywhere, in worship and praise we glorify and exalt the Lord. We rejoice and give thanks as we see God's "power at work within us" accomplishing God's redemptive mission for creation through God's people "abundantly far more than all we can ask or imagine" (3:20). As we join in mission together with all the saints, as God works in the world through us and many others, we and those with whom we labor will be "filled with all the fullness of God" (3:19). But we must always remember that this is not the goal. Mission and church are not ends in themselves. They exist for the glory of God.

"To [God] be glory in the church and in Christ Jesus to all generations, forever and ever. Amen" (3.21).

Act 4: Ephesians 4:1–16

The Connectedness of God's One Church-in-Mission

With the bridge word "therefore," chapter 4 introduces the second part of Ephesians. Building on the cosmic missional vision of chapters 1–3, which engages the church in spiritual and social realms, the author now develops a feet-on-the-ground holistic missional ecclesiology. What do life and ministry in a community of transformed disciples look like? The author begins by pleading with all baptized Christians to live our common calling "with all humility and gentleness, with patience, bearing with one another in love" (4:2). Unity and mission begin with and depend on these missional attitudes whereby we relate to others.[20] Only through humility, gentleness, patience, and bearing with one another in love can we be the church-in-mission. The Christian lifestyle is one of serving one another in harmonious relationships. I have been instructed and challenged by listening to the global church emphasize the vital importance of these attitudes in the issue of *Reformed World* on the theme "Unity of the Spirit in the Bond of Peace." It was issued in preparation for the meeting in 2010 where the World Alliance of Reformed Churches and the Reformed Ecumenical Council will unite. In an article in this journal, German pastor Sabine Dressler-Kromminga, whose story begins this chapter, comments on Ephesians 4:1–16:

Here Paul is not asking for the loving affection of everybody for everybody around or for some kind of enforced fondness; his point is not even about mutual understanding or tolerance. Here we are confronted with the very realistic apostolic view on relationships within the church, let alone personal relations: there are times when we can hardly stand each other. Sometimes it does not seem to be possible to stay in the same congregation or church with certain sisters and brothers. Various reasons—and some good ones might be amongst them—can call for separation, for breaking up, for continuing without the other. . . .

But our text admonishes us to do something different, to *bear with one another*, to stay instead of leaving, to work through all possible conflicts and to look at the counterpart through the eyes of God, trying to learn from Godly love for each creature.[21]

Ofelia Ortega and Marcos Cruz give further insights by looking at the opposites of humility, gentleness, and patience and applying them globally. Listen to them:

How much could we attain today in all fields of world politics and negotiations and in all spheres of human activity by refraining from pride, aggressiveness, and impatience? Ever since the times in which Paul took care of the Christian communities, these three virtues were associated with the attainment of unity and peace. How is humility to be interpreted in this globalizing and excluding world? A possible answer is that we are to set ourselves free from pride and arrogance, which create distances and divisions. Humility means the end of discriminatory attitudes of different forms. Outside the church, it contributes to bridge the gap not only between the poor and the rich, but also between North and South, women and men, black and white. It is present in all forms of struggle against discrimination, whether religious, political, social, or economic. Concerning the life and work of the church, humility lays the groundwork for its growth, paves the way for all forms of cooperation, and makes possible its spiritual wealth.[22]

Doing mission with others who are different from us requires humility, gentleness, patience, openness, mutual tolerance, and respect. It is necessary to intentionally refrain from pride, aggressiveness, and impatience. Our U.S. culture has indelibly impressed upon us attitudes that subvert some of our better characteristics, attitudes of arrogance, brazenness, competitiveness, discrimination, and selfishness, and the assumptions of superiority and empire building. We must find ways to free ourselves from our cultural captivity and honestly examine ourselves and our structures in light of these missional attitudes. It is not easy! This process begins, as Darrell Guder says, "with our confession that we need the Holy Spirit's continual work to convert us, and it continues as we approach Scripture, the traditions, and the global experiences of the church knowing that we always require forgiveness and renewal."[23]

Observe now these vital mission practices: "making every effort to maintain the unity of the Spirit in the bond of peace" (4:3). Unity and peace are gifts, accomplished facts produced by the Spirit, as well as tasks, disciplines, and mission practices. Unity and peace are the deepest longings and needs of humanity, commitments of all Christians and people of goodwill. "[Christ] is our peace" (2:14). Peace is well-being and security at every level. We long for peace within ourselves, in our churches, with other churches, and with other religions. So we must work for peace in a world broken by arrogance, violence, poverty, and injustice. We seek a visible, outward manifestation of church unity as well as an internal and organic pulsating of life in the one body of Christ. Argentine pastor Roberto Jordan says: "Unity involves true *koinōnia*, our coming together, seeing our differences, and still wanting to be at the service of God. There is no *koinōnia* in ignoring what we are and who we are in our differences. So when each of us sticks to our own personal views, to our own individual tradition, to our own set ways, unity of the Spirit will be hard to achieve."[24]

Our triune missionary God, who is breaking down barriers and who is creating one body, summons us to maintain, to preserve, to cultivate, to promote, to protect, to cherish "the unity of the Spirit" between and within churches. God comes to us graciously but asks for our collaboration. The Spirit works in and through us, but never forces us. The initial phrase "*making every effort to maintain the unity*" connotes eagerness and urgency. It is a continuous and diligent activity. We must work hard to resolve our difficulties and remove all that threatens our unity. We must build bridges that connect us rather than build barriers that separate us from our brothers and sisters. We must proactively reject any doctrine that legitimates sinful divisions in church and society. The church is called to be a unifying community, with unifying missional practices. We do mission better together!

Why is church unity so important? "There is one body and one Spirit, just as you were called to the one hope of your calling, one Lord, one faith, one baptism, one God and Father of all, who is above all and through all and in all" (4:4–6). Notice the repeated words "one" and "all" in these verses. Unity is based on the character of our one God. There is only one Christian church and one mission because there is only one triune God. Unity belongs to the church's identity as one body and one organic mission society. Unity and peace are vital in our effective witness to the world. Only a church that has peace can be an instrument of peace and a more humane alternative to chaos. Only a reconciled church can bear good news for all people. We worship and serve "one God and Father of all, who is above all and through all and in all" (4:6). There is an important missiological insight here. God's missionary action is inclusive. It surpasses the limits of the church. The fullness of God's mission is overwhelming. This is why our mission must be holistic. Any mission participant, local congregation, or denomination that neglects this wholeness is being less than what God intends it to be.

The unity in one Spirit, one body, and with one common mission is enriched by the diversity of gifts. We are all different. There is no uniformity. "Each of us was given grace according to the measure of Christ's gift" (4:7). Christ is Gift and, through the Holy Spirit who descended at Pentecost, is Giver of gifts. We are saved by grace and gifted by grace. With our gifts of grace, we come together in Christ. The amazing creativity and diversity of gifts and talents of God's people are part of the divine plan for the fullness of the church and of holistic mission. They are our manifold equipment for different ministries and tasks. However, diversity as richness presupposes cooperation. We need to learn to honor, respect, appreciate, and even encourage the impressive diversity of gifts and ministries in the church. Our partners around the world offer gifts of wisdom, discernment, prophetic boldness, hospitality, sensitivity, family togetherness, solidarity, human touch, simplicity, joy, and authenticity that make the disciplined practices of receptivity, observation, and openness so important. Do we really know how to affirm and receive the gifts of others? Congregations involved in mission long enough come to know that there are also severe problems in partner churches. Christians everywhere are capable of being wrong; just as we are shown forbearance at such times by many partners, we will have times when we have to be forbearing too.

In Ephesians 4:11 we discover that God has given gifts of leadership to some people in the body. To what end does God's church have leaders? "To equip the saints for the work of ministry, for building up the body of Christ, until all of us come to the unity of the faith, . . . to maturity, to the measure of the full stature of Christ" (4:12–13). We must grow up, mature, and join together in mission. It is an ongoing dynamic process. Unity leads to growth and maturity.

As G. B. Caird reminds us: "Only by the full exercise of these various gifts can the whole company of Christians grow together and . . . attain to a maturity which is not individual but communal."[25] Andrew Walls uses the metaphors in Ephesians to show that in the one church-in-mission, each member "is a building block belonging to a new temple still in process of construction . . . Each is an organ necessary to the proper functioning of a body under Christ's direction. Only together will they reach the fullness of Christ which is the completion and perfection of humanity."[26] Unity is an essential component of that maturity.

Equipping God's people is preparation for a task, for service of every kind, for participation in God's mission in the world. One of the most important challenges everywhere is "equipping the church for transforming mission," which builds up the global body of Christ. Mission workers, pastors, agencies, and professors offer mission education in the church today. The request that the PC(USA) receives most frequently from our partners is for "Developing Leaders" (a fourth core commitment in *Gathering for God's Future*); that makes empowering and enabling others an important role for mission coworkers, often working ourselves out of a job. I have accompanied this process, which involves pain on the part of mission coworkers but is a sign of the maturity and strength of human resources in our partner churches.

"But speaking the truth in love, we must grow up in every way into him who is the head, into Christ, from whom the whole body, joined and knit together by every ligament with which it is equipped, as each part is working properly, promotes the body's growth in building itself up in love" (4:15–16).

Though the literal translation is "truthing in love," there are enough references to "speaking" later in Ephesians for me to stop and notice the importance of the practice of intentional listening to and hearing what others are saying, especially those in the South. What are they saying? Claudio Carvalhães from the Independent Presbyterian Church of Brazil wrote a meditation on a Waldensian Oath titled "Louder Please, I Can't Hear You: Voices, Spiritualities, and Minorities" in which he asks: "Can we move beyond the pleasurable tone of our voices and hear the voice of the other?" He refers to voices that have been "historically dismissed and forbidden" and to "different voices that speak a 'foreign' theological language." He says: "The ability to listen to somebody else's voice is the opening of the Spirit within us to 'see' God's movements in unexpected people and places."[27] It is precisely these voices speaking truths that are sometimes hard for us to hear and accept. Needless to say, we both speak and listen in love.

As members of one local and global Christian community, we find direction and depth in our journey toward fullness and maturity in this exhortation: "We must grow up in every way into him who is the head, into Christ" (v. 15). The adverbial phrase "in every way" means literally "the whole." It is holistic growth of the whole person and the whole church. However, the word "the whole" or "all things" is used in Ephesians 1:10 to show the scope of God's missional gathering: the cosmos. It also is used in reference to God's putting "all things" under Christ, making him head "over all things for the church," and to Christ, who "fills all in all" (1:22–23; 4:10). So growing up "in every way" is not merely about the internal spiritual growth of Christians and churches. It is also about growing in our holistic missional vision and outreach, which obtains cosmic dimensions. God's mission restores the whole person, the whole church, the whole inhabited earth, and the whole universe.

Keep going and meditate on the phrase "the whole body, joined and knit together" (4:16). Try to visualize a huge jigsaw puzzle or huge tapestry representing the wholeness of the church in all its diversity "joined and knit together." Not only do parts of the body fit together in harmony or in covenant; they also are knit or kept together by mutual instruction and mission. Use your human anatomy imagination now: "joined and knit together by every ligament with which it is equipped." Ligaments are connections. Touch with gratitude some of your own "connecting joints" that piece your body together and keep it moving. Ralph Martin underlines the importance of these joints: "It is through 'every joint' (or ligament or connection) that the entire body is compacted and unified; and each part is supplied with a connecting joint. . . . The head and each part must cooperate. To enable 'each part' to work as it should, the intermediary 'joints' play a vital role in the analogy."[28] We need these connectors in the church to help link us together in mutual dependence, trust, and open communication. Who are the connectors in your church, agency, mission group, and denomination?

The body is a living organism in relationships that grows into full maturity for mission in union with Christ only when "each part is working properly" in harmony with the rest. When I asked my colleague Timothy Carriker about this verse, he commented, "To answer your question, I think '*every* ligament' and '*each* part' refer to the plurality of the parts of the whole body (the church). In the analogy, the ligaments and parts are not the same pieces, but serve different functions. Both, however, are pluralities. . . . The body has many ligaments, not just one, that keep the (other) parts together."[29]

Many of us have the gifts and vital roles as "connectors" or "intermediary joints" that build connections and enable each "part" of the church-in-mission to work properly in cooperation and complementarity with other parts. Furthermore, we need connecting structures in the local, national, and universal church. When "each part is working properly," the result is "the body's growth in building itself up in love" (4:16). This whole section begins and ends "in love." Without love, all that we do in church and mission is "a noisy gong or a clanging cymbal" (1 Cor. 13:1).

In the search for the unity and connectedness in mission envisioned in Ephesians, I find inspiration as I listen to Claudio Carvalhães, who ends his essay on the Waldensian Oath with these words:

So, as one and multiple communities, with different faces, colors, voices, bodies, classes, ears and tongues, springing a variety of spiritualities and experiences with God, it is our task to create a hospitable community that is marked by diversity. . . . The voice of God is plural, received and spoken not by one major voice but by many voices. It is among our differences, voices, and languages that we can loudly say:

Joining our hands,
Let us LOUDLY proclaim,
At the altars of my God,
So I want to live and to die![30]

Act 5: Ephesians 4:17–6:20

Conflicts within God's Church and World

The last three chapters of the Letter to the Ephesians, beginning with 4:17, show the down-to-earth reality of some of the tensions and conflicts in the growing churches. After the sublime visions of God's cosmic mission and of the unity of God's church-in-mission, we need a reality check. Within Christians, within churches, between churches, and in the greater world, we find conflicting values, traditions, and behaviors. We don't always live out what we profess to be in our baptisms. The church is not yet what God intends it to be. In our networks of social relationships and in the structures and institutions of church and society, gospel values and attitudes do not always prevail. At times there are bitter confrontations, clashes, and deep divisions.

In these verses of Ephesians, words pile up to show the nature of these tensions and conflicts: "futility," "darkened understanding," alienation from God, "ignorance and hardness of heart," "loss of sensitivity," sexual immorality, "greed," "obscene silly and vulgar talk," foolishness, and frivolity (some terms recast). We deal with "falsehood," stealing and corruption in myriad forms, with "bitterness and wrath and anger and wrangling and slander, together with all malice" (4:31). These are real tensions, real conflicts, real confrontations, real contradictions; and they are very close to us, even within us. The media bombards us constantly. All of us are vulnerable. There are multiple and conflicting understandings even of unity and mission. On a regular basis we live with tensions and confrontations.

These verses serve as a somber and realistic warning to all of us. We live in a world where the boundaries between truth and lies, good deeds and evil deeds, constructive words and destructive words often blur. Motives seem always to be mixed. Evil all around and within suffocates, alienates, and even paralyzes us. It reminds us of what Jesus said when he sent the seventy in mission: "I am sending you out like lambs into the midst of wolves" (Luke 10:3). We are challenged to speak words of grace and truth (Eph. 4.25, 29), "to share with the needy" (4:28), to build one another up (4:29), and to "live as children of light" in a world of much darkness (5:8). We must divorce ourselves from certain attitudes and actions that contradict the values of the gospel of love, peace, and justice that we proclaim. We are warned and instructed: "Be careful then how you live, not as unwise people but as wise, making the most of the time, because the days are evil. So do not be foolish, but understand what the will of the Lord is" (5:15–17). Don't wander aimlessly through life's maze. Our call is to conscientiously "wake up" (5:14), actively "stand against" (6:11), and constantly "pray" and "keep alert" (6:18). The Holy Spirit's role in giving us discernment, resistance, and power is emphatic: "Be filled with the Spirit" (5:18). The wisdom and empowerment of the Spirit are essential.

In all times the church exists in a world of tensions and conflicting relationships and structures. Jesus and the leaders in the early church lived in a climate of domination and oppression by the Roman Empire. Patriarchy and slavery were accepted cultural institutions and empire values. The writer of Ephesians speaks about relationships between husbands and wives, parents and children, masters and slaves. Since this section should be read as a unit, I find it most helpful to begin with the situation of masters and slaves. The writer cannot obliterate the existing cultural context, but the underlying gospel principle is clear: "You know that both of you have the same Master in heaven, and with him there is no partiality" (6:9). Obviously, we do not use these verses to support slavery today. In like manner, the writer does not deny the existing cultural hierarchy and patriarchy, but as did Jesus, he offers the gospel principles of mutual love and submission: "Be subject to one another out of reverence for Christ" (5:21). Obviously, we do not use these verses to support domination of any kind today. Mutuality and dialogue are very important gospel principles in all relationships.

Ephesians significantly ends with a poignant recognition of the church's struggle "against the rulers, against the authorities, against the cosmic powers of this present darkness, against the spiritual forces of evil" (6:10–20). These verses are part of the larger section on human and social relationships, tensions, and conflicts. The church's interpretations of these powers vary from "spiritual warfare" to "unjust societal structures." Both interpretations have much to teach us. Our battle, like our mission, is *both* in spiritual and social-historical realms. It is part of the cosmic struggle against the forces of evil, which has been portrayed in many series of books and movies, such as

Star Wars, Harry Potter, Chronicles of Narnia, and the Lord of the Rings trilogy. It is no surprise that a mission with cosmic dimensions involves a battle of cosmic dimensions.

However, this final somber section begins on an encouraging note: "Be strong in the Lord and in the strength of his power" (6:10). This takes us back to where we started in Ephesians 1:10 with our Creator God, who is Sovereign over all the powers of the cosmos. Yes, the first and last words are God's! For this reason, it is only through much prayer, hope, confidence in God's power, and firm grounding in "the word of God" (6:17) that we move forward in God's mission. It is not merely with our own material, intellectual, strategic, or spiritual resources that we engage in God's mission, but with God's own "armor." Allegorical language is used to portray "the whole armor of God" (vv. 11, 13): truth, the practice of justice, the proclamation of the gospel of peace, faith, salvation, and the word of God (vv. 14–17). Holistic mission requires holistic preparation and holistic divine resources! God's armor enables the church to overcome the powers and corrupting forces in our hostile world.

The final section of Ephesians ends, appropriately, with the first and final order of the day in mission: Pray! Pray! Pray! After the moving prayers in Ephesians 1:15–23 and 3:14–21 comes the final exhortation: "Pray in the Spirit at all times in every prayer and supplication. To that end keep alert and always persevere in supplication for all the saints" (6:18). Missional prayer is all-inclusive, local and global, personal and corporate, holistic, cosmic, and ecumenical. So, Pray! Pray! Pray!

Chapter 5

Some Final Thoughts

"An event of planetary dimensions" or "the coronation of a king without a crown" is the way some described the inauguration of Barack Hussein Obama as president of the United States of America on January 20, 2009. Nearly two million exuberant people, mostly youth, filled the Mall in Washington while billions around the world followed the event. Ecstatic crowds in Nairobi, Kenya, proudly accompanied the steps of their latest hero.

Following the eighteen-minute inaugural address, commentators poured forth their reactions. One in Brazil observed that the address was a surprising contrast to the imperial scenery of the event. With no pomp or arrogance, Obama's address was marked by humility and realism. He admitted fear of the decline of the United States. It was a message of peace and tolerance, including the Islamic world. He spoke a word of hope and dignity to the poor. Hailed as the first president-celebrity, the new generation Blackberry president, he acknowledged the multicultural and multireligious nature of the country. Given the African and Muslim heritage of his fathers, the world perceives this as a giant step in breaking down many walls of prejudice. Hopefully, a new era of dialogue and cooperation will prevail over violence and force. Those who chose Obama as recipient of the Nobel Peace Prize, nine months after his inauguration, demonstrated their belief in this new style of international diplomacy. His response, basically, was: "I am surprised, humbled, and challenged."

The world has changed drastically. The new millennium began on September 11, 2001, when four commercial airplanes hijacked by Islamic terrorists demolished the World Trade Center towers in New York City, damaged the Pentagon in Washington, and went down in Pennsylvania, with the sacrifice of many innocent victims. People around the globe responded in solidarity and hoped for a united spirit of multilateralism against world terrorism. They were disappointed and angered by the unilateral attack and long war in Iraq. The world changed again in September 2008, when the real estate bubble burst in the United States, with foreclosures unprecedented since the Great Depression. The domino effect of a credit crisis in banks and financial institutions in the United States, Europe, and Japan and faltering stock markets soon made it evident that Wall Street would never be the same. Recession soon appeared.

Again leaders of growing emergent economies like Brazil, Russia, India, China, and South Africa, as well as many civil society and church activists, hope for cooperation in long-overdue, radical reforms leading to a new and more just global economic order. The creation of the United Nations after World War II was a global attempt to avoid the eruption of a Third World War (in which it succeeded). Similarly, the meeting of the G-20[1] in London in May 2009 was a multilateral global attempt to avoid the eruption of another international financial crisis. For the first time in modern history, the voices of the seven strongest economies (G-7) no longer dominate and impose. Emerging economies now have an important voice and contribution.

Indeed, the economic crisis is an opportunity to move beyond unilateralism, protectionism, individualism, competition, greed, waste, and excesses— to move onward and practice the good stewardship of our human, material, and natural resources. It is a moment to recognize the equality of all nations. Yes, it is better to work together against terrorism, to regulate world commerce, and to promote a green economy in order to preserve the planet.

Why am I saying all of this in the conclusion of a book about holistic mission? I learned in Ephesians that the fullness of God's mission includes both the spiritual and the sociohistorical realms. God transforms persons and structures. We do mission with "the Bible in one hand and the newspaper in the other" (attributed to Karl Barth). We study the text and the context. Re-visioning holistic mission in partnership leads us to rethink evangelism, compassionate service, politics, economy, ecology, and global relationships. Local and global mission are affected by the relationships between nations in our globalized world. Arab Christians in the Middle East ardently seek negotiated peace. Presbyterians in Cuba yearn for the freedom of all Americans and Cubans to travel and trade bilaterally. Presbyterians in Colombia plead with the U.S. government to invest more in humanitarian aid and human rights and less in military aid and bases, which has not improved their situation. My perspective on the war against terrorism, the present economic crisis, and the expectations surrounding Obama is of a bicultural missiologist who lives and is immersed in the Southern hemisphere and closely connected to the PC(USA).

I recently witnessed the change that has transpired in the global church. Three partner churches of the PC(USA)—the Independent Presbyterian Church of Brazil, the Presbyterian Church of Ghana, and the Presbyterian

Church of Egypt—gathered in Brazil in February 2009 for a consultation on Cross-Cultural Mission. The Ghanaians have much cross-cultural mission within their country, with so many dialects. One of the pastors uses four languages in the liturgy in his megachurch. For the Egyptians, cross-cultural mission means getting out of the country in a Christian witness to peace in the Muslim world. Brazilians do cross-cultural mission in the diverse regions of their country of continental dimensions and with Portuguese speakers in the United States, Portugal, Angola, and Mozambique. The Brazilian denomination invited both the Presbyterian Church in Ghana and in Egypt to enter into bilateral partnerships with them. What a joy to see the expanding South-South mission partnerships and leadership in sending cross-cultural missionaries.

The extensive celebrations of Edinburgh 2010 will mirror the changes in the global church and the directions for world mission in the twenty-first century. The centenary of the Edinburgh 1910 World Missionary Conference is an intercontinental and multidenominational venture. Participants come from the whole range of Christian traditions and confessions worldwide. The polycentric approach—with events in many locations around the world, including Edinburgh—is indicative of the increasing decentralization in our globalized society in a multicentric Christian church. The church in the Global South, barely represented in 1910, is now the majority church in the world and the leader and prophetic voice in 2010. Mission leaders from the older and new mission movements of the North join in respectful and creative dialogue with the new mission movements in the South and the East, to jointly discern God's direction for the future. Networks, global alliances, mission practitioners, agencies, and scholars must be mobilized to develop greater strategic collaboration and synergy in holistic mission.

Voices from representative world Christianity today in Africa and Latin America pose difficult questions. Lamin Sanneh, professor at Yale University, teases us into thinking seriously with his book *Whose Religion Is Christianity?*[2] Philip Jenkins helped people in the pews begin to understand what African scholars like Sanneh and Kwame Bediako have been saying: "The era of Western Christianity has passed within our lifetimes, and the day of Southern Christianity is dawning." Jenkins further says that "members of a Southern-dominated church are likely to be among the poorer people on the planet . . . , more conservative in terms of both beliefs and moral teaching,"[3] and Pentecostal or charismatic.

In other words, representative Christianity has again become what it was originally: a non-Western religion. Many Northern observers and participants in mission are slow to accept this phenomenon, to engage this trend, and to see its practical implications. The changing roles and images of mission participants are greater than most people realize. This requires fresh insights and profound thinking for all of us.

Phyllis Zoon is a Presbyterian pastor in New Jersey who participated in two short-term mission trips to Bolivia with the Presbyterian Hunger Program. Challenged by her brief mission experiences, she invited former PC(USA) mission workers in Bolivia, Bob and Julie Dunsmore, to speak in her presbytery. Bob explained that the glaciers in Bolivia provide water for millions of people yet may be gone within ten years because of global warming. Phyllis, inspired by Bob's presentation, experienced a moment of transforming mission-in-reverse. "Bob told us that what we can do to help our brothers and sisters in Bolivia the most is not writing a check or even sending clothing or medicine," she said.[4] "Their biggest request is that we drive less. Our partners in Bolivia say that what they most want is for us to change the way we live so that we can at least mitigate the effects of climate change. It's a whole new way of doing mission because it asks us not to give so they can live like us but to change, to transform our lives so they can live."

As a result, Phyllis began to modify her behavior! "Their appeal that we change ourselves [has] changed me," she said. "I have started putting fewer pollutants into the air, I buy less stuff, and I've gotten more involved in local initiatives and in the environment than ever before. I'm preaching the message broadly throughout the presbytery that the small changes we can each make in our own lives can have a big impact." To make and advocate lifestyle changes, Phyllis has used *Just Eating? Practicing Our Faith at the Table*,[5] a PC(USA) curriculum that facilitates dialogue about our daily eating habits, the Christian faith, and the "needs of the broader world."

She also encourages participation in the Presbyterian Coffee Project, which helps to ensure that more of Americans' "coffee dollar" goes to the farmers who do the work. "This is something that people can do," Phyllis Zoon said. "These are changes that we can make in our lives. We can give up the cup of coffee that we buy and make a gourmet cup of fair trade coffee at home. We can really do these things so that our lives will be changed, all while we learn the stories of the people behind the different projects." This is rethinking holistic mission. "So often we give our money so people can be like us when they don't really want that," she said. "We think we can do things in the short term without changing our own long-term behavior. But Jesus came into the world to change lives, starting with our own."

As we consider the global food crisis, energy crisis, and forthcoming water crisis, significant parts in God's holistic mission for us can be driving, wasting, and eating *less* so that all can eat and the planet can survive. Zoon's story can help us discover some of the lost pieces in the great puzzle of God's cosmic mission!

I started this book by talking about my practices of healthy eating and regular walking as parts of a holistic lifestyle. In the course of writing and reflecting on holistic mission, I discovered that my eating and walking, like my weekly participation in the Eucharist, are both symbolic and real experiences of God's mission of fullness of life.

Christian mission is participation in the missionary dialogue of the triune God of love, which overflows in dialogue with others in mission and with all of God's creatures. We seek communion in relationships and communion in mission. We cannot rush into mission enthusiastically without first learning the disciplines of listening and reflection. In our zeal we cannot neglect the freedom and dignity of all human beings, nations, and the peoples of the world's cultures. The only road to fullness, wholeness, and togetherness in mission is authentic *dialogue.*

Mission and planetary survival in the new millennium will require much humility, patience, dialogue, discipline, and partnership! Our triune God models all of this for us. Missionary dialogue and rethinking the relationship of the different pieces of the big picture of God's mission are vital today. Diversity was built into creation and into the church forever. Surely this diversity is a delight to our Creator. So, it should not be a problem for us. Our different ministries belong to a single mission. All of our mission work as individuals, local congregations, or as mission agencies is incomplete and partial; complete mission is found only in the fullness of God's holistic mission. There are now an infinite number of parts, participants, and places in God's mission. They include people doing frontier evangelism, others meeting urgent health and housing needs, others advocating social and economic justice and the preservation of natural resources. Many work with denominational agencies; others are sent by local congregations or specialized mission groups. Some minister in their own cities; others cross national and cultural borders.

God's Spirit is breaking down the walls that divide all these diverse mission agents and locations and uniting all of us in the rich fullness of God's local-global holistic mission. To God be the glory now and forever!

Appendix A

A Study Guide for Group Reflection and Practice

*T*his study guide can be utilized by group leaders or individuals to discern and participate in God's holistic mission together.

Chapter 1: What Is Mission Today?

Many Parts, One Mission: Integrating Evangelism, Compassion, and Justice

Opening Images and Questions

1. Bring to class a large jigsaw puzzle, either assembled, with certain sections assembled, or unassembled. Encourage people to work on the puzzle until class begins. Discuss the following questions: What is the best way to assemble a puzzle with many parts? In what ways is God's mission like a puzzle with many parts? Is it better to assemble a thousand-piece jigsaw puzzle together with others or individually? Why? Could we do mission better together? Why? How willing are you to engage in mission cooperatively?

2. Present an example of the harmonious and loving relationship of the Trinity by reading a brief portion from *The Shack*, by William P. Young.

3. Bring three balls and see how people do with juggling them.

4. Have available copies of newsletters of several PC(USA) mission workers in various countries and ask people to comment on what kind of mission activity they see in each letter (www.pcusa.org/missionconnections).

Readings and Questions for Reflection

1. What comes to your mind when you hear the word *mission?* What is mission today for you? What images surface when you hear the word *holistic?*

2. Ask four people to read aloud the following texts: Matthew 25:34–40; Matthew 28:18–20; Luke 4:18–19; Luke 24:45–49.

3. Divide into three groups. Give each group figure 1.1 from chapter 1, newsprint, and markers.

Group 1: Place at the top of the newsprint the word EVANGELISM and list ways you and your congregation and related mission groups practice evangelism.

Group 2: Place at the top of the newsprint the word COMPASSIONATE SERVICE and list ways you and your congregation and related mission groups practice compassionate service.

Group 3: Place at the top of the newsprint the word SOCIAL JUSTICE and list ways you and your congregation and related mission groups practice social justice.

4. Ask each group to present their lists. Display them side by side for all to see.

5. Discuss the following questions: Where do you see points of over-lap, integration, and convergence? With which aspect of mission do you most identify? What did you learn from the aspect that is most difficult for you? What does it mean to be holistic in mission? How can we become more holistic?

Mission Dialogue and Practice

1. How can people who engage in one aspect of mission encourage and enter into a respectful missionary dialogue with groups engaged in other aspects?

2. Have you experienced cooperation and dialogue with mission partners different from you? Share your experience.

3. Can you think of ways your congregation can seek more dialogue and collaboration with others in mission?

Missional Prayer

Close with a reading of Ephesians 4:1–6 and a few minutes of silent reflection for self-critique and identification of your blind spots. Ask God's Spirit to give you the courage and honesty to name and admit your sinful attitudes and to actively resist attitudes of individualism, fragmentation, compartmentalization, and judging. Make a commitment to missionary dialogue. Begin that adventure by praying for one person or group whose understanding of and participation in mission differs from yours.

Chapter 2: Who Is Engaged in Mission Today?

Many Participants in God's Mission: Expanding Partnerships

Opening Images and Questions

1. What comes to your mind when you hear the word "partnership"?

2. How important is the Internet to you? What is the purpose of social networks?

3. List on the board the mission groups and programs you remember from this chapter. If technology permits, do some Presbyterian mission Internet surfing. Begin with www.pcusa.org. Go to world mission and links. Include www.missioncrossroads.ning.com, a PC(USA) country network, and www.pcusa.org/calltomission.

3. If you do not have this technology in class, make copies of some of the home pages of these organizations or gather materials on them from the church office. Allow members to select one and complete the following: "The thing that strikes me in this is _____."

4. Discuss the questions at the beginning of the chapter: How are all the players connected? How do we expand our partnerships? Why is it important for groups within the PC(USA) to do mission together? Can diverse mission groups promote unity and overcome competition in the PC(USA)? How can Presbyterian Frontier Fellowship, Presbyterian Global Fellowship, and Presbyterian Peace Fellowship join hands as partners in mission? Why is it sometimes easier for us to work with our global partners than with each other in our own ecclesial body? What is our changing role in the greater global church? How do we become more ecumenical?

5. Bring pictures of the human skeletal system, a box of Lego building blocks, and/or a plant with many branches. Talk about the relationships and connections between the parts in each.

Listening to God's Word and Reflecting

1. Read 1 Corinthians 12:4–31, with emphasis on verses 6 and 7: "There are varieties of activities, but it is the same God who activates all of them in everyone. To each is given the manifestation of the Spirit for the common good." What does this passage say about cooperation and connections in the body of Christ? The gifts and body parts mentioned in the chapter can apply to individual Christians or to groups committed to specific mission activities. How should we treat the multiple mission groups in our denomination? How do we participate in mission as part of a global community of faith, as well

as individual mission practitioners? Why does the chapter end pointing to "a still more excellent way"?

2. Read Ephesians 4:11–16. What is the function of a ligament in the body? Comment on the importance of being "joined and knit together" in the global church's mission today. How can we overcome barriers and do mission together? What could you do in your congregation to promote expanding partnerships in mission?

Mission Dialogue and Practice

1. If you are involved in a mission partnership individually or collectively as a congregation, presbytery, or denomination, candidly evaluate your practice of the principles in "Presbyterians Do Mission in Partnership" (www .pcusa.org/worldwide/get-involved/partnership.htm):

- Shared grace and thanksgiving
- Mutuality and interdependence
- Recognition and respect
- Open dialogue and transparency
- Sharing of resources

2. Encourage your congregation to sign "An Invitation to Expanding Partnership in God's Mission" (www.pcusa.org/calltomission/pdf/invitation.pdf).

Missional Prayer

1. Read Philippians 2:6–8. Reflect on the statements that Christ Jesus "emptied himself" and "humbled himself." Consider your attitudes, especially when material resources are unevenly owned.

2. Share stories of occasions when you participated in missionary dialogue and collaboration with other mission initiators and partners. Remember ways your denominational mission agency facilitates your participation in global mission. Offer prayers for these mission agents.

Chapter 3: Where Is the Location of Mission Today?

Many Places in God's Mission: Local-Global Synergy

Opening Images and Observations

1. Sit in a circle to help build community and promote interconnectedness and equal opportunity to be seen and heard. As an opening ritual, ask people

to offer thanks to God for one gift your congregation has given to the local community and one gift it has received from local or global partners. Place a reminder of God's presence at the center, maybe a candle, a city map, and a world globe.

2. Ponder the globe and talk about the changes that have taken place now that the majority global faith community is in the Southern hemisphere and is very active in mission and growing considerably.

3. Invite a guest from a local ecumenical or community organization to share examples of reaching out with compassion and social justice in the community.

4. Invite an international guest or two in the community to dialogue about how they have been received in church and community and what they have to offer to the church and community. Ask them to share their faith journeys, the mission work of churches in their home country, and the challenges they have faced as immigrants or refugees.

Listening to God's Word and Reflecting:

1. Read Luke 4:14–16, 31, 42–44; Acts 1:8; 28:16, 30–31; Romans 15:22–29. Use a map to locate Judea, Samaria, Galilee, Jerusalem, Nazareth, Capernaum, Rome, and Spain. (In Luke 4:44 some manuscripts read "Judea" while others give the more logical "Galilee.") What do these passages say to you about local-global? The Gospel writers show that both Jesus and Paul had a strong sense of place in relation to their mission. In Luke, Jesus starts his ministry in Nazareth of Galilee, his hometown, and in 9:51 begins his journey to Jerusalem. Acts 1:8 is a strategic plan of the movement in the entire book. The church begins in Jerusalem. Like Jesus, the early church moves out, while never abandoning the home base. Jesus remains in Palestine but demonstrates a concern for mission to Gentiles. Paul is the leading missionary to the Gentiles, but he never loses hope for the salvation of Israel. Read Romans 15:22–29 out loud again. How does this text help you to understand mission-in-reverse or two-way mission? Why do you think Paul was set on returning to Jerusalem even while knowing that it was dangerous for him? Why was Paul so eager to reach Rome and Spain?

2. Read Luke 10:29–37 and 17:11–19. The healing of the ten lepers happens on the borders of Samaria and Galilee. Who are the heroes in the two stories? What do you know about the Samaritans? They were a marginalized culturally and ethnically mixed group that, for nationalistic Jews, were worse than Gentiles and considered to be nonhumanity. What do these texts say to us today?

Mission Dialogue and Practice

Use the four guidelines of the interaction of the axes of global-local and sending-receiving presented in the chapter and the questions below to evaluate the mission activity of your local congregation. Discuss how you can apply these in practical ways.

1. *Congregations do local mission outside the front door with an awareness of the presence of the global community near and far, with a special concern for least reached and marginalized peoples, and with a perception of the global implications of all issues.*

What mission is your congregation doing in your "backyard," neighborhood, city, and county? Who are the invisible groups of people in your community? Are you welcoming and building relationships with people from all nations in your community?

2. *Congregations participate in God's universal mission around the world in partnership with the global church, with an awareness of least reached and marginalized peoples, and with maximum respect, solidarity, mutuality, and hands-on involvement.*

What global mission engagement does your congregation support? Remember short-term mission trips as well as long-term partnerships or mission personnel. Do humility, respect, reciprocity, mutuality, and solidarity characterize this involvement?

3. *Congregations receive the global community locally, from near and far, as God's gifts and missionary agents to them.*

What services and gifts have your congregation received from persons from other countries now living in your country? Is your local community multicultural? Is your congregation? Why or why not?

4. *Congregations experience the global church internationally and allow Christian messages, values, and practices learned from brothers and sisters in other contexts to continually nurture and transform them.*

What have you learned from Christians from other countries? Give concrete examples of how your values and understanding, attitudes, and practice of mission have been transformed by your international experiences. Remember ways your mission partners have taught you. How is your local congregation being transformed?

Missional Prayer

Close in a literal or symbolic way that further builds community among you. Pray for those in your community and in the world who experience marginalization. Pray the following prayer together:

Creator God,
may the power of your gospel and transforming mission
be at work in our community and church
and in every country in the world
today and always. Amen.

Chapter 4: What Does the Bible Say about Mission?

One Holistic Mission: A Biblical and Theological Reflection on Ephesians

Opening Images and Questions

1. Imagine yourself, your local congregation, and the global church on a journey toward fullness and maturity. What do the phrases "in every way" or "all things" or "the whole" or "fullness" mean on this journey? How is mission related to the holistic growth of the whole person and the whole church? Breathe slowly and deeply as you ponder these phrases: Christ "fills all in all" (Eph. 2:22–23; 4:10) and "so that you may be filled with all the fullness of God" (3:19). What do these phrases mean to you, to the church, and to the universe?

2. Bring pictures to class that illustrate the terms "cosmic" and "planetary." Observe them and think about the scope of God's cosmic mission. What does God's mission gather and restore?

3. Meditate on this phrase: "the whole body, joined and knit together" (4:16). Try to visualize a huge jigsaw puzzle or tapestry representing the wholeness of the church in all its diversity "joined and knit together." What makes the parts of the body fit together in harmony?

4. Use your human-anatomy imagination: "joined and knit together by every ligament with which it is equipped." Ligaments are connections. Touch with gratitude some of your own "connecting joints" that piece your body together and keep it moving. Who are the connectors in your church, mission agency/group, and denomination?

Readings and Questions for Reflection

1. Provide a handout to each person with the following texts: Ephesians 1:3–14, 20–23; 3:9–11. Ask each person to read the texts silently and encircle all the words or phrases that describe God's missional *plan*, as well as the uses of the word "all." Allow people to share what they have learned about the content and scope of God's mission. What metaphors or analogies help unpack the phrase "wisdom of God in its rich variety" (3:10)?

2. Read and discuss Ephesians 2:13–22. God creates in Christ "one new humanity" (v. 15). Christ gives us peace and reconciliation. Mission begins by *breaking down dividing walls* between Christians (v. 14). What does this mean? What walls are we building rather than breaking down in the church? How do you feel about being "joined together" (v. 21) in one missional community of reconciled differences? What does it require of you and your congregation? What are your problems and fears? How can mission groups who are quite different or distant do mission together?

3. Read Ephesians 4:1–16 and discuss the following questions. What is the significance for mission of the words "one" and "all" in verses 4–6? What is the importance of unity in and for mission? How do you understand the role of Christ's gifts to the church in mission today? What is the importance of the phrase "as each part is working properly" in verse 16?

Mission Dialogue and Practice

1. A key verse in Ephesians is "a plan for the fullness of time, to gather up all things" in Christ (1:10). If "gathering together" or "summing up" or "causing convergence" is a key in God's missionary action in the universe, what are the implications for churches today? How do we join in gathering for God's future? (Provide copies of the PC(USA) document *Gathering for God's Future: Witness, Discipleship, Community; A Renewed Call to Worldwide Mission.*)

2. Describe all the ways in which your local congregation, presbytery, and denomination participate in God's cosmic mission of environmental preservation and planetary survival.

3. What are some practical ways in which missionary dialogue between churches, mission initiators, and people from diverse cultures enables us to bear "with one another in love, making every effort to maintain the unity of the Spirit in the bond of peace" (4:2–3)?

4. Think of ways that you might practice dialogue and unity, beginning in this class today, in your local congregation, in your town, in your work and ministry, in your denomination, and in wider circles.

5. In groups or as a class, create and present a diagram, chart, work of art with paint or play dough, litany, confession of faith, prayer, liturgical dance, role play, pantomime, drama, or song that demonstrates unity in God's mission.

Missional Prayer

Close by placing the prayer in Ephesians 3:14–21 on a poster, board, transparency, or slide. Allow members of the class to spontaneously use phrases from the text to formulate their prayers. After each prayer, use as a group response: "To God be the glory."

Appendix B

An Invitation to Expanding Partnership in God's Mission

As members of the Presbyterian Church (USA) committed to God's mission, accompanied by global partners, we gathered together January 16–18, 2008, in Dallas, Texas.[1] We acknowledge the rich Presbyterian heritage in world mission and reaffirm the Presbyterian understanding of God's mission as it is expressed in *Gathering for God's Future* [2003]:

> *The Good News of Jesus Christ is to be shared with the whole world. As disciples of Jesus Christ, each of us in the Presbyterian Church (U.S.A.) is sent into the world to join God's mission. As individuals and as a church, we are called to be faithful in this discipleship. Our mission is centered in the triune God. Our mission is God-called, Christ-centered and Spirit-led. Our mission is both proclamation and service; it is the reason the church exists. . . .*
>
> *Our renewed call from God is to face the challenges of witnessing and evangelizing worldwide, equipping the church for transforming mission, engaging in ministries of reconciliation, justice, healing, and grace, and living the Good News of Jesus Christ in community with people who are poor, [persecuted, and living in the midst of violence]. . . .*
>
> *The church is part of God's plan. We are called into the community of the church, and we call new disciples into that community. With Christ as our head, the church community exists for the sake of God's mission. We learn to serve in mission in a way that is faithful to the triune God. We are to model the kind of community [that] God intends for all humanity. To be the church is to be one large mission society.[2]*

Grounded in this theological foundation, we realize that God is calling us to new patterns of mission. The world has changed, and the majority of the world's Christians are now in Latin America, Africa, and Asia.

The great growth and mission faithfulness of the Church outside the West invite us into a new posture. We must listen and learn to receive. We must also be open to new patterns of collaboration. These new patterns involve new cooperation and partnerships within the PC(USA).

I.   We recognize that God calls us to mission that is grounded in confession of our sins, grows out of a life of prayer, and is sustained in worship. Therefore, we covenant to live and serve together in God's mission according to the following *values*:
1. Trusting in the Holy Spirit and trusting in one another as each discerns how God is moving us in mission. (Acts 10)
2. Doing mission in the way of Jesus, who humbled himself, showing the way of self-giving and self-emptying. (Philippians 2)
3. Seeking to be faithful to God as we live and proclaim the fullness of Jesus Christ's good news; personal witness to those outside the church, justice for the oppressed, and compassion for those in need. We accompany others in their efforts to be faithful. (Luke 4)
4. Affirming the complementary nature of God's gifts to all in the one body of Christ and encouraging one another in living out those gifts. (1 Corinthians 12)
5. Recognizing our responsibility to each other by communicating openly, acting transparently, and speaking and hearing the truth in love. (Ephesians 4)
6. Striving in our mission to be aware of the context out of which we come, to respect the persons with whom we labor, and to honor the context in which they live. In an era of massive global inequalities, we commit ourselves to be sensitive to and address the issues of power that result from our differences. (Philippians 2)
7. Valuing long-term relationships, partnerships characterized by perseverance, and long-term commitments which support and encourage global partners. (1 Thessalonians 2)

II. We seek to live out these mission values with humility, integrity, and steadfastness. Recognizing that God invites us all to be full participants in God's mission, we commit ourselves to *work cooperatively* with one another in the following ways:
1. We will affirm and encourage World Mission as it continues to move from a regulatory role to a more enabling and equipping role.
2. We will celebrate and encourage diverse Presbyterian approaches and structures for mission while maintaining the unity of our participation in God's mission.
3. We will share responsibility for the education and preparation of all Presbyterians for mission.

4. We commit ourselves to seeking more mission personnel who will serve long-term in cross-cultural contexts through the PC(USA), and to supporting them fully.
5. We commit ourselves to enabling and supporting our global partners as they send their mission personnel in cross-cultural service.
6. We recognize and affirm the growing opportunity for cross-cultural mission in our own increasingly pluralistic and multi-cultural society, and we receive the global community from near and far as mission partners and God's gift to us. We seek increased integration between local and global mission.

III.   As we move forward together in God's mission, we commit ourselves to calling the church to ongoing intercessory *prayer* for God's mission and to the following *tasks*:
1. We will form a Coordinating Committee to ensure that we will meet together to share and cooperate on a regular basis.
2. During the coming year we will work to address two immediate priorities:
   a. to coordinate and collaborate in the sending of mission personnel.
   b. to expand Presbyterian funding for mission personnel.
3. During the next three months we will share this document and invitation with our constituencies.

IV.   With bold humility we *invite* those who would covenant with us to join in this new collaborative model of Presbyterian mission, and we ask for encouragement, for guidance and for prayer, remembering Jesus' own prayer:

The glory that you have given me I have given them, so that they may be one, as we are one, I in them and you in me, that they may become completely one, so that the world may know that you have sent me and have loved them even as you have loved me. (John 17:22–23)

We, the undersigned, as individuals, join in the covenant, and we will encourage the organizations we serve to affirm it as well. Signed this January 18, 2008.

Consultation Participants

Carol Adcock	Paul Friesen	Lien Nguyen
Anne Barstow	Sue Fricks	Setri Nyomi
Marilyn Borst	Sherron George	K. T. Ockels
Will Browne	Joan Gray	James Oudom

Vernon Broyles
Barbara Campbell-Davis
Nancy Cavalcante
Tae Su Cheong
Carol Clarke
Patricia Cuyatti
John Daniel
Enos Das Pradhan
David Dawson
Don Dawson
Enock De Assis
Lionel Derenoncourt
Paul Detterman
Hunter Farrell
Ann Ferguson
Judia Foreman

Tim Hart-Andersen
Jo Ella Holman
Rhashell Hunter
Francie Irwin
Cliff Kirkpatrick
Karla Koll
David Kpobi
Sara Lisherness
Tricia Lloyd-Sidle
Victor Makari
Kathy Matsushima
Mike McCormick Huentelman
Milton Mejia
Jim Milley
Dave Moore
Rachel Morris

Greg Roth
Bill Simmons
Dale Stanton-Hoyle
Ellie Stock
Scott Sunquist
Tom Taylor
Rick Ufford-Chase
Linda Valentine
Scott Weimer
Rob Weingartner
Doug Welch

Jim Wilson
Bill Young
Jake Young
Maria Zack

These Signers Represented Groups Engaged in Global Mission, Including

Advisory Committee on the Constitution
Association of Presbyterian Mission
    Pastors
General Assembly Council (PC(USA))
Joining Hands Against Hunger
Medical Benevolence Foundation
Mission Directors from Large
    Congregations
Mission Networks, PC(USA)
Mission Professors from PC(USA)
    Seminaries
New Wilmington Mission Conference
Office of the General Assembly, PC(USA)
The Outreach Foundation
Pastors from Immigrant Churches
Pastors from Large Congregations
PC(USA) Young Adult Volunteers
    Program

Peace and Justice, PC(USA)
Presbyterian Frontier Fellowship
Presbyterian Global Fellowship
Presbyterian Mission
    Co-Workers
Presbyterian Peace Fellowship
Presbyterian Women
Presbyterians for Renewal
Presbytery Partnerships
Racial, Ethnic, and Women's
    Ministries, PC(USA)
Relief and Development,
    PC(USA)
Witherspoon Society
World Mission, PC(USA)
World Mission Initiative

Joined by Global Partners from

Colombia, Ghana, India, Peru, and Vietnam

Notes

FOREWORD BY HUNTER FARRELL

1. Robert J. Priest, Terry Dischinger, Steve Rasmussen, and C. M. Brown, "Researching the Short-Term Missionary Movement," *Missiology* 34, no. 4 (2006): 477–95.

PREFACE

1. I realize that most Christians think that Paul wrote the Letter to the Ephesians. Scholars are rather evenly divided. I could change my mind, but presently I think that it was written by a second-generation Christian who built on and further developed Paul's thoughts, especially his ecclesiology, and used Paul's name to give authority and credibility. This was common at that time. However, the question of authorship and date are secondary. The important thing is what the epistle teaches us.

CHAPTER 1: WHAT IS MISSION TODAY?

1. Orlando Costas, *The Integrity of Mission* (San Francisco: Harper & Row, 1979), 75.

2. C. René Padilla, "The Fullness of Mission," in *Mission between the Times: Essays on the Kingdom* (Grand Rapids: Wm. B. Eerdmans Publishing Co., 1985), 141.

3. José Míguez Bonino, *Faces of Latin American Protestantism*, trans. Eugene L. Stockwell (Grand Rapids: Wm. B. Eerdmans Publishing Co., 1997), 140–43.

4. David J. Bosch, *Transforming Mission: Paradigm Shifts in Theology of Mission* (Maryknoll, NY: Orbis Books, 1995), 399. This is the basic book I recommend to all pastors and mission workers. For those who find it too dense, see Stan Nussbaum, *A Reader's Guide to Transforming Mission*, a concise, accessible companion to David Bosch's classic book (Maryknoll, NY: Orbis Books, 2005).

5. Bosch, *Transforming Mission*, 512.

6. "Inculturation" is a specialized mission studies term used especially by Roman Catholics. Protestants often use "contextualization" as an equivalent. These terms refer to the way the gospel message takes on distinctive expressions in each culture.

7. Stephen B. Bevans and Roger P. Schroeder, *Constants in Context: A Theology of Mission for Today* (Maryknoll, NY: Orbis Books, 2005), 394.

8. Andrew Walls and Cathy Ross, eds., *Mission in the Twenty-first Century: Exploring the Five Marks of Global Mission* (Maryknoll, NY: Orbis Books, 2008), xiv–xv.

9. Figure 1.1, "God's Holistic Mission" (with some revisions), and much of the material that follows is from my chapter "Faithfulness through the Storm: Changing Theology

of Mission," in *A History of Presbyterian Missions, 1944–2007*, ed. Scott W. Sunquist and Caroline Becker (Louisville, KY: Geneva Press, 2008), 85–109, esp. 103ff.

10. *The Constitution of the Presbyterian Church (U.S.A.)*, Part II, *Book of Order* (Louisville, KY: Office of the General Assembly, 2001), G-3.0300c.

11. Ibid., G-3.0300b.

12. Donal Dorr, *Mission in Today's World* (Maryknoll, NY: Orbis Books, 2000), 195.

13. Stephen Knisely, *Faith in Action: Understanding Development Ministries from a Christian Perspective* (Louisville, KY: Presbyterian Church (U.S.A.), 2001), 39.

14. *Constitution*, Part II, *Book of Order*, G-3.0300c3c.

15. See www.christianpost.com/article/20071001/29529_Survey:_Top_Issues_of_Concern_for_American_Evangelicals.htm.

16. John R. W. Stott, *Christian Mission in the Modern World* (Downers Grove, IL: InterVarsity Press, 1975), 27.

17. Padilla, "The Fullness of Mission," 197–98.

18. Vera White, *Hand in Hand: Doing Evangelism and Doing Justice* (Louisville, KY: Presbyterian Peacemaking Program, 1991), 1.

19. William P. Young, *The Shack: Where Tragedy Confronts Eternity* (Newbury Park, CA: Windblown Media, 2007).

20. Robert Zwetsch, *Missão como com-paixão* (São Leopoldo, RS, Brazil: Editora Sinodal, 2008).

21. Clinton M. Marsh, *Evangelism Is . . .* (Louisville, KY: Geneva Press, 1997), 71.

22. World Council of Churches, *Mission and Evangelism: An Ecumenical Affirmation.* A study guide for congregations (New York: Division of Overseas Ministries and National Council of the Churches of Christ in the U.S.A., 1983), par. 34.

23. Bosch, *Transforming Mission*, 483.

CHAPTER 2: WHO IS ENGAGED IN MISSION TODAY?

1. This program was originally called the Joining Hands Against Hunger initiative (JHAH), but the last two words were dropped and it became simply Joining Hands (JH). It is not related and should not be confused with the churchwide fund-raising campaign called "Joining Hearts and Hands."

2. These groups will be explained later in the chapter.

3. Sherron Kay George, *Called as Partners in Christ's Service: The Practice of God's Mission* (Louisville, KY: Geneva Press, 2004), 1.

4. Bonino, *Faces of Latin American Protestantism*, 141.

5. Shirley C. Guthrie says we are "unlikely partners," "junior partners," and "servant partners" who "share in God's saving and renewing work in the world"; *God for the World— Church for the World: The Mission of the Church in Today's World* (Louisville, KY: Witherspoon Press, 2000), 34–37. This is an excellent six-session study guide for churches.

6. "Presbyterians Do Mission in Partnership," Louisville, KY: Presbyterian Church (USA), adopted by the 215th General Assembly (2003), www.pcusa.org/worldwide/get-involved/partnership.htm.

7. In *Partnership, Solidarity, and Friendship: Transforming Structures in Mission*, A study paper for the PC(USA) (Louisville, KY: Worldwide Ministries Division, Presbyterian Church (U.S.A.), 2003), Philip L. Wickeri gives a historical review of the discussions on partnership. The seeds were planted at the International Missionary Council (IMC) in Jerusalem in 1928, and the concept became more specific at the IMC meeting at Whitby, UK, in 1947 with

the theme "partners in obedience." It was further elaborated in 1952 at the IMC in Willingen, Germany, from the perspective of *missio Dei*. Wickeri (9) contends that "there has been no real development of the ideas of partnership in mission since [the] Bangkok" Assembly of the WCC's Commission on World Mission and Evangelism in 1972.

8. Wickeri, *Partnership, Solidarity, and Friendship*, 4.

9. Milton J. Coalter, John M. Mulder, and Louis B. Weeks, *Vital Signs: The Promise of Mainstream Protestantism* (Grand Rapids: Wm. B. Eerdmans Publishing Co., 1996), 98–99. In this chapter they further show how "parachurch groups" have moved into the breach. They conclude the chapter by saying: "The challenge before the emerging denomination is to forge a compelling theological vision and sufficiently flexible organizational structures—those that will allow the creativity of the congregations to flourish in communion with other congregations, rather than to languish alone" (101). Westminster/John Knox Press (Louisville, KY) published the full results of the study in seven volumes in the series The Presbyterian Presence: The Twentieth-Century Experience. The seventh volume, Milton J. Coalter, John M. Mulder, and Louis B. Weeks, *The Re-Forming Tradition: Presbyterians and Mainstream Protestantism* (1992), is also a summary. There the authors clearly state: "The congregation is now the locus of power and mission in American Presbyterianism" (113).

10. Pat Cole, "'An Enormous Phenomenon': Scholar Estimates That 2 Million U.S. Christians Travel Abroad Annually on Short-Term Mission," News: Presbyterian News Service, Louisville, KY, October 2, 2008, www.pcusa.org/pcnews/2008/08718.htm.

11. "Guidelines for WMD-Related 'Mission Networks,'" Internal document of Ecumenical and Mission Partnerships, Worldwide Ministries Division, Presbyterian Church (U.S.A.), Louisville, KY: February 2004.

12. Brad and Ali Kent, "Bolivia: They Came, They Saw, They Connected," *Joining Hands Newsletter*, Tenth Edition, June 2009, www.relufa.org/partners/jhnewsletter/bolivia.htm; Alexandra Buck, "Peru: What Fair Trade Looks Like from Down Here," and other articles in this issue of *Joining Hands Newsletter*, Tenth Edition, June 2009, "www.relufa.org/partners/jhnewsletter/peru.htm.

13. Peru Mission Network site, February 28, 2009, reporting the mission statement adopted in January 2009, www.perumissionnetwork.com/index.php?news&nid=3.

14. Stanley H. Skreslet, "Networking, Civil Society, and the NGO: A New Model for Ecumenical Mission," *Missiology* 25, no. 3 (July 1997): 308–9.

15. Rob Weingartner, "Missions within the Mission: New Diversities in the One Family," in Sunquist and Becker, *A History of Presbyterian Missions*, 110.

16. Ibid., 130.

17. "Presbyterians at Work around the World" (2009), www.pcusa.org/worldwide/get-involved/networks.htm.

18. See "Mission Crossroads PC (USA)," www.missioncrossroads.ning.com.

19. Paul E. Pierson, "Beyond Sodalities and Modalities: Organizing for Mission in the Twenty-first Century," in *Evangelical, Ecumenical, and Anabaptist Missiologies in Conversation*, ed. J. R. Krabill, W. Sawatsky, and C. E. Van Engen (Maryknoll, NY: Orbis Books, 2006), 233.

20. Ibid.

21. See Darrell L. Guder's essay "Missional Connectedness: The Community of Communities in Mission," the last chapter in *Missional Church: A Vision for the Sending of the Church in North America* (Grand Rapids: Wm. B. Eerdmans Publishing Co., 1998). He says the local congregation is a primary agent in mission, but not in isolation. We need connecting

structures that provide a "missional connectedness for the universal church in all its diversity"; "the connecting structures are crucial to the nature of the church as the people of God for God's mission" (249). Furthermore, he says that catholicity demands attention to "the relationship, or lack of it," between denominational structures and local or specialized agencies; "for the sake of missional integrity, these diverse agents of mission need to move toward each other in dialogue" (258).

22. Andrew Kirk in *What Is Mission?* (Minneapolis: Fortress Press, 2000) reminds us that "one particular aspect of partnership is the position occupied by agencies within the Church which are not directly linked to the Churches' formal structures" (198). He suggests that such voluntary agencies must constantly wrestle with the following questions: loyalties, openness to other Christians, accountability, duplication, and long-term commitment; they must ultimately seek "co-operation in mission" (199–201).

23. World Council of Churches, "Most Diverse Christian Gathering Ever to Discuss Unity and Common Witness," News Release, November, 5, 2007, 193.73.242.131/pressreleasesen .nsf/index/pr-07-76.html. See Konrad Raiser, *Ecumenism in Transition*, trans. Tony Coates (Geneva: WCC Publications, 1991).

24. World Council of Churches, "Let's Take Risks, Kobia Tells Global Christian Forum," News Release, November 7, 2007, www2.wcc-coe.org/pressreleasesen.nsf/index/pr-07-77.html.

25. World Council of Churches, "'Historic Breakthrough'—Global Christian Forum to Go Forward, Extending an Invitation to Join the Encounter," News Release, November 12, 2007, www2.wcc-coe.org/pressreleasesen.nsf/index/pu-07-28.html.

26. Ibid.

27. Ibid.

28. See the complete document in Appendix B. To add your name to the list of endorsers, visit www.pcusa.org/calltomission. Some of the following information comes from Toya Richards Hill, "Diverse Presbyterian Groups Develop Core Values for Mission," *Highlights*, Spring/Summer 2008, Presbyterian World Mission, Louisville, KY.

29. *Gathering for God's Future: Witness, Discipleship, Community; A Renewed Call to Worldwide Mission*, adopted by the 215th General Assembly, 2003 (Louisville, KY: Worldwide Ministries Division, PC(USA), 2003).

30. World Communion of Uniting Churches, "Uniting General Council, www.reformed churches.org.

31. "Unity of the Spirit in the Bond of Peace: The Uniting General Council of the World Communion of Reformed Churches" is the title of *Reformed World* 58, nos. 2–3 (June–September 2008), warc.jalb.de/warcajsp/news_file/revistafinal.pdf. This issue of *Reformed World*—published by the World Alliance of Reformed Churches (WARC) in Geneva—is preparation for the Council in June 2010 in Grand Rapids, Mich., when WARC and the Reformed Ecumenical Council will unite. The theme for that council will be from Eph. 4: "Unity of the Spirit in the Bond of Peace." The eleven articles in this issue are reflections on the theme and have been very instructive to me in my reflections on Ephesians. I will quote several of the articles in chap. 4.

32. Wickeri, *Partnership, Solidarity, and Friendship*, 21–22, 27–28.

33. I talk about the practice of mutual receiving and giving and gift exchange in *Called as Partners*, 73–76. In a communication to the moderators/conveners of PC(USA) Mission Networks, Hunter Farrell said the following: "One of the biggest problems in congregational twinning projects, presbytery partnerships, and other mission partnerships (including church-

to-church partnerships at the national level!) is that all of us are tempted to think that money is the key to personal and societal transformation. When we put it in such stark terms, of course, we would all maintain this isn't the case, but often our relationships have been built around financial, rather than human, resources. This shaping of mission relationships around money means all of us (Christians from the Global North *and* the Global South) tend to expect North American Christians to be the givers (because they generally have greater financial resources) and Christians from the Global South to be the receivers (because they generally have fewer financial resources). It's not about money and, in fact, money is often one of the greatest barriers to mission (Jonathan Bonk's *Missions and Money* [see n. 37 below] raises disturbing, but important, issues around this subject)." I would add that those of us from the Global North need desperately to learn to be receivers and to accept those from the Global South as givers. See also chap. 10, "The Changing Uses of Money: From Self-support to International Partnerships," in Michael Pocock, Gailyn Van Rheenen, and Douglas McConnell, *The Changing Face of World Missions: Engaging Contemporary Issues and Trends* (Grand Rapids: Baker Academic, 2005), which begins by saying, "Money is a two-edged sword—it can either empower or hinder missionary efforts" (279). They show many of the problems of mission workers operating out of affluence, as well as harmful short-term mission gifts. One solution is to strictly pursue the goal of responsible self-supporting churches with no more money from outside. Another option is the development of authentic international partnerships based on trust, equality, relationships, accountability, and mutual complementation in which U.S. mission agencies employ national missionaries to help the churches in their own countries provide structures to become mission-sending movements. Andrew Walls says: "Relationships so easily become finance-dominated; it is hard to keep relations on an equal footing when the regular topic of conversation is money, and how much"; see *The Missionary Movement in Christian History* (Maryknoll, NY: Orbis Books; Edinburgh: T&T Clark, 1996), 253. René Padilla in "The Fullness of Mission" says: "The possibility of reciprocal giving between churches is a basic premise without which no healthy relationship between rich and poor churches is attainable. . . . Giving and receiving cannot be maintained unless there is between the churches a mature relationship based on the gospel" (137). A further complication is that the term "donor control" can be read in both directions. Sometimes the financial resources of the "richer partner" are welcomed, their presence is tolerated, but their input to plans and directions are often rejected, ignored, or seemingly resented. The issue is indeed complex.

34. Wickeri, *Partnership, Solidarity, and Friendship*, 3.

35. Ibid.

36. See Segundo Galilea, *Responsabilidade missionária da América Latina*, trans. José Américo Coutinho (São Paulo, Edições Paulinas, 1983), 29–40. Also his chapter "A Missão aos Pobres, a Partir dos Pobres e de Nossa Pobreza," in *A Missão a partir da América Latina*, trans. Eugênia Flavian (São Paulo, Edições Paulinas, 1983), 143–53.

37. See Jonathan J. Bonk, *Missions and Money: Affluence as a Western Missionary Problem* (Maryknoll, NY: Orbis Books, 1991).

38. As a mission coworker in Guatemala, Dennis Smith gave a penetrating talk titled "Do No Harm," demonstrating some of the problems affluence can cause. See excerpts at www.brentwoodfirstpresbyterian.org/documents/contemporaryreflection.pdf.

39. Kirk, *What Is Mission?* 201.

40. Hunter Farrell, letter to World Mission Louisville staff and mission personnel, March 6, 2009.

CHAPTER 3: WHERE IS THE LOCATION OF MISSION TODAY?

1. Art Beals, *When the Saints Go Marching Out! Mobilizing the Church for Mission* (Louisville, KY: Geneva Press, 2001), 17.

2. Ibid., 14, quoting the Mission Handbook of University Presbyterian Church.

3. Ibid., 22.

4. Figure 3.1, "Local-Global Mission Partners and Challenges," is from my article "Local-Global Mission: The Cutting Edge," *Missiology* 28, no. 2 (April 2000): 192–94. It was also used in *A History of Presbyterian Missions*, 108. Used with permission from *Missiology*.

5. Coalter, Mulder, and Weeks, *The Re-Forming Tradition*, 113.

6. Clifton Kirkpatrick, "The Unity of the Church in Mission," address given in St. Louis in November 1997, in *Congregations in Global Mission: New Models for a New Century*, a conference report by Worldwide Ministries (Louisville, KY: Office of Global Awareness and Involvement, Worldwide Ministries Division, Presbyterian Church (U.S.A.), 1998), 5.

7. Marian McClure, "Dichotomy Busters," address given in St. Louis in November 1997, in *Congregations in Global Mission: New Models for a New Century*, a conference report (Louisville, KY: Worldwide Ministries Division, Presbyterian Church (U.S.A.), 1998), 83–86.

8. Robert J. Schreiter, *Constructing Local Theologies* (Maryknoll, NY: Orbis Books, 1985), 2, 4.

9. Bevans and Schroeder, *Constants in Context*, 1.

10. Schreiter, *Constructing Local Theologies*, 11. See Vincent Donovan, *Christianity Rediscovered* (Maryknoll, NY: Orbis Books, 1982).

11. Philip Jenkins, *The Next Christendom: The Coming of Global Christianity* (New York: Oxford University Press, 2002), 2; a revised and updated edition came out in 2007.

12. Ian T. Douglas, "Globalization and the Local Church," in *The Local Church in a Global Era: Reflections for a New Century*, ed. Max L. Stackhouse, Tim Dearborn, and Scott Paeth (Grand Rapids: Wm. B. Eerdmans Publishing Co., 2000), 204.

13. Philip Jenkins, *The New Faces of Christianity: Believing the Bible in the Global South* (New York: Oxford University Press, 2006).

14. Robert J. Schreiter, *The New Catholicity: Theology between the Global and the Local* (Maryknoll, NY: Orbis Books, 1997).

15. Leonardo Boff, *A Trindade e a sociedade*, 5th ed. (Petropolis: Vozes, 1999), 192.

16. Leonardo Boff, *Civilização planetária: Desafios à sociedade e ao cristianismo* (Rio de Janeiro: Sextante, 2003).

17. Douglas, "Globalization and the Local Church," 205.

18. The four summary points and comments are adapted from the section "Local-Global Symbiosis" in my article "Local-Global Mission," 192–94.

19. Schreiter, *The New Catholicity*, xi.

20. Figure 3.2, "The Local-Global Symbiosis," is fig. 2 in the *Missiology* article cited in note 18 and is used here with permission.

21. *Gathering for God's Future*, 8.

22. Schreiter, *The New Catholicity*, 124–27.

CHAPTER 4: WHAT DOES THE BIBLE SAY ABOUT MISSION?

1. Sabine Dressler-Kromminga, "What Unity Requires on the Road to 'World Communion of Reformed Churches,'" *Reformed World* 58, nos. 2–3 (June–September 2008): 148, warc.jalb.de/warcajsp/news_file/revistafinal.pdf.

2. Bosch, *Transforming Mission*, 496.

3. Figure 4.1, "God's Mission in the Bible," updates and revises the second part of fig. 1 from my chapter in *A History of Presbyterian Missions*, 104.

4. Marian McClure, "The Top Ten Reasons to Put the Great Commission at the Heart of Your Ministry," unpublished paper, Louisville, KY, 2000.

5. Ralph P. Martin, *Ephesians, Colossians, and Philemon*, Interpretation: A Bible Commentary for Teaching and Preaching (Atlanta: John Knox Press, 1991), 17.

6. John R. W. Stott, *The Message of Ephesians*, The Bible Speaks Today (Leicester, UK: Inter-Varsity Press; Downers Grove, IL: InterVarsity Press, 1979), 64–65.

7. Michael Downey, *Altogether Gift: A Trinitarian Spirituality* (Maryknoll, NY: Orbis Books, 2000), 43.

8. Ibid., 43, 56, 57–58.

9. Carola Tron, "Water and the Christian Community in a Liquid Modernity—a Latin-American Perspective," *Reformed World,* 57, no. 1 (March 2007): 38, warc.jalb.de/warcajsp/news_file/RWMarch2007.pdf.

10. Walls, *The Missionary Movement in Christian History*, 25.

11. Walls and Ross, *Mission in the Twenty-First Century*, 204.

12. Ofelia Ortega and Marcos Cruz, "United in Search for a Fair Peace," *Reformed World* 58, no. 2–3 (June–September 2008): 126, warc.jalb.de/warcajsp/news_file/revistafinal.pdf.

13. Samuel P. Huntington, *The Clash of Civilizations and the Remaking of World Order* (New York: Simon & Schuster, 1996).

14. Stott, *The Message of Ephesians*, 110.

15. Ibid., 102.

16. Andrew F. Walls, *The Cross-Cultural Process in Christian History* (Maryknoll, NY: Orbis Books, 2002), 69.

17. Timóteo Carriker, *Proclamando boas novas: Bases sólidas para o evangelism* (Brasília: Editora Palavra, 2008), 36.

18. Ibid., 43.

19. *Gathering for God's Future*, 16.

20. Part 2 of my book *Called as Partners in Christ's Service* has three chapters on the missional attitudes of respect, compassion, and humility.

21. Dressler-Kromminga, "What Unity Requires," 147.

22. Ortega and Cruz, "United in Search for a Fair Peace," 129–30.

23. Guder, *Missional Church*, 267.

24. Roberto Jordan, "Unity of the Spirit in the Bond of Peace: Called to Make Every Effort," *Reformed World* 58, nos. 2–3 (June–September 2008): 154, warc.jalb.de/warcajsp/news_file/revistafinal.pdf.

25. G. B. Caird, *Paul's Letters from Prison*, New Clarendon Bible (Oxford: Oxford University Press, 1984), 71.

26. Ibid., 204.

27. Claudio Carvalhães, "Louder Please, I Can't Hear You: Voices, Spiritualities and Minorities," *Reformed World* 57, no. 1 (March 2007): 43, 47, 49, warc.jalb.de/warcajsp/news_file/RWMarch2007.pdf.

28. Martin, *Ephesians, Colossians, and Philemon*, 54.

29. I am grateful to my colleague Timothy Carriker, who in e-mail conversations shared his insights on these translations in Ephesians. He uses Ephesians 3 and 4 to build a biblical basis for evangelism in his book *Proclamando boas novas*. Many of his insights have guided

my missiological reading of Ephesians. Timothy is professor of missions at the service of the Independent Presbyterian Church of Brazil and has served the Presbyterian Church (U.S.A.) as a mission coworker in Brazil for over three decades.

30. Carvalhães, "Louder Please, I Can't Hear You," 56.

CHAPTER 5: SOME FINAL THOUGHTS

1. Created in 1999, the G-20 is a group that gathers the top finance and bank representatives of 19 countries—Germany, South Africa, Saudi Arabia, Argentina, Australia, Brazil, Canada, China, South Korea, United States, France, India, Indonesia, Italy, Japan, Mexico, Great Britain, Russia, Turkey—plus a European Union representative. It supersedes the former G-7—Germany, Canada, United States, France, Italy, Japan, and Great Britain—plus Russia.

2. This question comes from the title of the book by Lamin Sanneh, *Whose Religion Is Christianity? The Gospel beyond the West* (Grand Rapids: Wm. B. Eerdmans Publishing Co., 2003).

3. Jenkins, *The Next Christendom*, 3, 2, 7.

4. This story and all of the citations are taken from "A Whole New Way of Doing Mission," by Emily Enders Odom, in Presbyterian News Service, Presbyterian Church (USA), Louisville, KY, April 27, 2009, www.pcusa.org/pcnews/2009/09342.htm.

5. Jennifer H. Schrock, *Just Eating? Practicing Our Faith at the Table*, curriculum produced by the Presbyterian Hunger Program, Advocate Health Care and Church World Service (Louisville, KY: Presbyterian Church (USA), 2005).

APPENDIX B: INVITATION TO EXPANDING PARTNERSHIP

1. This statement was produced and endorsed by the participants of the Presbyterian Church (U.S.A.) mission consultation in Dallas, Texas, January 16–18, 2008, and endorsed by the General Assembly in 2008. It is a public document: www.pcusa.org/calltomission/pdf/invitation.pdf.

2. *Gathering for God's Future*, 1, 16, with added text in brackets.

Bibliography

Beals, Art. *When the Saints Go Marching Out! Mobilizing the Church for Mission*. Louisville, KY: Geneva Press, 2001.

Bevans, Stephen B., and Roger P. Schroeder. *Constants in Context: A Theology of Mission for Today*. Maryknoll, NY: Orbis Books, 2005.

Boff, Leonardo. *A Trindade e a sociedade*. 5th ed. Petropolis: Vozes, 1999. ET, *Trinity and Society*. Translated by Paul Burns. Maryknoll, NY: Orbis Books, 1988.

———. *Civilização planetária: Desafios à sociedade e ao cristianismo*. Rio de Janeiro: Sextante, 2003.

Bonino, José Míguez. *Faces of Latin American Protestantism*. Translated by Eugene L. Stockwell. Grand Rapids: Wm. B. Eerdmans Publishing Co., 1997.

Bonk, Jonathan J. *Missions and Money: Affluence as a Western Missionary Problem*. Maryknoll, NY: Orbis Books, 1991.

Bosch, David J. *Transforming Mission: Paradigm Shifts in Theology of Mission*. Maryknoll, NY: Orbis Books, 1991.

Caird, G. B. *Paul's Letters from Prison*. New Clarendon Bible. Oxford: Oxford University Press, 1984.

Carriker, Timóteo. *Proclamando boas novas*. Brasília: Editora Palavra, 2008.

Carvalhães, Claudio. "Louder Please, I Can't Hear You: Voices, Spiritualities and Minorities." *Reformed World* 57, no. 1 (March 2007): 45–57, warc.jalb.de/warcajsp/news_file/RWMarch2007.pdf.

Coalter, Milton J., John M. Mulder, and Louis B. Weeks. *The Re-Forming Tradition: Presbyterians and Mainstream Protestantism*. The Presbyterian Presence: The Twentieth-Century Experience 7. Louisville, KY: Westminster/John Knox Press, 1992.

———. *Vital Signs: The Promise of Mainstream Protestantism*. Grand Rapids: Wm. B. Eerdmans Publishing Co., 1996.

The Constitution of the Presbyterian Church (U.S.A.), Part II, *Book of Order*. Louisville, KY: Office of the General Assembly, 2001.

Costas, Orlando. *The Integrity of Mission*. San Francisco: Harper & Row, 1979.

Donovan, Vincent. *Christianity Rediscovered*. Maryknoll, NY: Orbis Books, 1982.

Dorr, Donal. *Mission in Today's World*. Maryknoll, NY: Orbis Books, 2000.

Douglas, Ian T. "Globalization and the Local Church." In *The Local Church in a Global Era: Reflections for a New Century*, edited by Max L. Stackhouse, Tim Dearborn, and Scott Paeth, 202–8. Grand Rapids: Wm. B. Eerdmans Publishing Co., 2000.

Downey, Michael. *Altogether Gift: A Trinitarian Spirituality*. Maryknoll, NY: Orbis Books, 2000.

Dressler-Kromminga, Sabine. "What Unity Requires on the Road to 'World Communion of Reformed Churches.'" *Reformed World* 58, nos. 2–3 (June–September 2008): 143–50, warc .jalb.de/warcajsp/news_file/revistafinal.pdf.

Galilea, Segundo. *A missão a partir da América Latina*. Translated by Eugênia Flavian. São Paulo: Edições Paulinas, 1983.

———. *Responsabilidade missionária da América Latina*. Translated by José Américo Coutinho. São Paulo: Edições Paulinas, 1983.

Gathering for God's Future: Witness, Discipleship, Community; A Renewed Call to Worldwide Mission. Adopted by the 215th General Assembly, 2003. Louisville, KY: Worldwide Ministries Division, Presbyterian Church (U.S.A.), 2003.

George, Sherron Kay. *Called as Partners in Christ's Service: The Practice of God's Mission*. Louisville, KY: Geneva Press, 2004.

———. "Local-Global Mission: The Cutting Edge." *Missiology* 28, no. 2 (April 2000): 187–97.

Guder, Darrell L. *Missional Church: A Vision for the Sending of the Church in North America*. Grand Rapids: Wm. B. Eerdmans Publishing Co., 1998.

Guthrie, Shirley C. *God for the World—Church for the World: The Mission of the Church in Today's World*. Louisville, KY: Witherspoon Press, 2000.

Jenkins, Philip. *The New Faces of Christianity: Believing the Bible in the Global South*. New York: Oxford University Press, 2006.

———. *The Next Christendom: The Coming of Global Christianity*. New York: Oxford University Press, 2002.

Jordan, Roberto. "Unity of the Spirit in the Bond of Peace: Called to Make Every Effort." *Reformed World* 58, nos. 2–3 (June–September 2008): 151–62, warc.jalb.de/warcajsp/ news_file/revistafinal.pdf.

Kirk, J. Andrew. *What Is Mission?* Minneapolis: Fortress Press, 2000.

Kirkpatrick, Clifton. "The Unity of the Church in Mission." In *Congregations in Global Mission: New Models for a New Century*, a conference report by Worldwide Ministries. Louisville, KY: Office of Global Awareness and Involvement, Worldwide Ministries Division, Presbyterian Church (U.S.A.), 1998.

Knisely, Stephen. *Faith in Action: Understanding Development Ministries from a Christian Perspective*. Louisville, KY: Presbyterian Church (U.S.A.), 2001.

Marsh, Clinton M. *Evangelism Is . . .* Louisville, KY: Geneva Press, 1997.

Martin, Ralph P. *Ephesians, Colossians, and Philemon*. Interpretation: A Bible Commentary for Teaching and Preaching. Atlanta: John Knox Press, 1991.

McClure, Marian. "Dichotomy Busters." In *Congregations in Global Mission: New Models for a New Century*. A conference report. Louisville, KY: Worldwide Ministries Division, Presbyterian Church (U.S.A.), 1998.

———. "The Top Ten Reasons to Put the Great Commission at the Heart of Your Ministry." Unpublished paper: Louisville, KY, 2000.

Nussbaum, Stan. *A Reader's Guide to Transforming Mission*. A concise, accessible companion to David Bosch's classic book. Maryknoll, NY: Orbis Books, 2005.

Ortega, Ofelia, and Marcos Cruz. "United in Search for a Fair Peace." *Reformed World* 58, nos. 2–3 (June–September 2008): 123–34, warc.jalb.de/warcajsp/news_file/revistafinal.pdf.

Padilla, René. *Mission between the Times: Essays on the Kingdom*. Grand Rapids: Wm. B. Eerdmans Publishing Co., 1985.

Pierson, Paul E. "Beyond Sodalities and Modalities: Organizing for Mission in the Twenty-first Century." In *Evangelical, Ecumenical, and Anabaptist Missiologies in Conversation*, edited by J. R. Krabill, W. Sawatsky, and C. E. Van Engen, 225–34. Maryknoll, NY: Orbis Books, 2006.

Pocock, Michael, Gailyn Van Rheenen, and Douglas McConnell. *The Changing Face of World Missions: Engaging Contemporary Issues and Trends*. Grand Rapids: Baker Academic, 2005.

"Presbyterians Do Mission in Partnership." Louisville, KY: Presbyterian Church (U.S.A.), adopted by the 215th General Assembly, 2003. www.pcusa.org/worldwide/get-involved/partnership.htm.

Raiser, Konrad. *Ecumenism in Transition*. Translated by Tony Coates. Geneva: WCC Publications, 1991.

Sanneh, Lamin. *Whose Religion Is Christianity? The Gospel beyond the West*. Grand Rapids: Wm. B. Eerdmans Publishing Co., 2003.

Schreiter, Robert J. *Constructing Local Theologies*. Maryknoll, NY: Orbis Books, 1985.

———. *The New Catholicity: Theology between the Global and the Local*. Maryknoll, NY: Orbis Books, 1997.

Skreslet, Stanley H. "Networking, Civil Society, and the NGO: A New Model for Ecumenical Mission." *Missiology* 25, no. 3 (July 1997): 308–9.

Stott, John R. W. *Christian Mission in the Modern World*. Downers Grove, IL: InterVarsity Press, 1975.

———. *The Message of Ephesians*. The Bible Speaks Today. Leicester, UK: Inter-Varsity Press; Downers Grove, IL: InterVarsity Press, 1979.

Sunquist, Scott W., and Caroline Becker, eds. *A History of Presbyterian Missions, 1944–2007*. Louisville, KY: Geneva Press, 2008.

Tron, Carola. "Water and the Christian Community in a Liquid Modernity—a Latin-American Perspective." *Reformed World* 57, no. 1 (March 2007): 31–44, warc.jalb.de/warcajsp/news_file/RWMarch2007.pdf.

Walls, Andrew F. *The Cross-Cultural Process in Christian History*. Maryknoll, NY: Orbis Books, 2002.

———. *The Missionary Movement in Christian History*. Maryknoll, NY: Orbis Books; Edinburgh: T&T Clark, 1996.

Walls, Andrew F., and Cathy Ross, eds. *Mission in the Twenty-first Century: Exploring the Five Marks of Global Mission*. Maryknoll, NY: Orbis Books, 2008.

Weingartner, Rob. "Missions within the Mission: New Diversities in the One Family." In *A History of Presbyterian Missions, 1944–2007*, edited by Scott Sunquist and Carolina Becker, 110–31. Louisville, KY: Geneva Press, 2008.

White, Vera. *Hand in Hand: Doing Evangelism and Doing Justice*. Louisville, KY: Presbyterian Peacemaking Program, 1991.

Wickeri, Philip L. *Partnership, Solidarity, and Friendship: Transforming Structures in Mission*. A study paper for the PC(USA). Louisville, KY: Worldwide Ministries Division, Presbyterian Church (U.S.A.), 2003.

World Council of Churches. *Mission and Evangelism: An Ecumenical Affirmation*. A study guide for congregations. New York: Division of Overseas Ministries and National Council of the Churches of Christ in the U.S.A., 1983.

Young, William P. *The Shack: Where Tragedy Confronts Eternity*. Newbury Park, CA: Windblown Media, 2007.

Zwetsch, Roberto. *Missão como com-paixão*. São Leopoldo, RS, Brazil: Editora Sinodal, 2008.